Whether it's through college, everyday life, or careers, the importance of taking care of oneself is paramount. That's the focus of Nurturing Our Self: During College, Everyday Life And The Job Search, a treatise on how to care for one's psyche when life changes demand new directions.

The pandemic has forced many to deviate (sometimes widely) from their set careers, objectives, and views of life. Thus, there's perhaps no better time to consult Nurturing Our Self, which focuses on how to self-nurture through a variety of stressful experiences.

Positivity starts inside ourselves and spreads outward. This requires a basic change in mindset, from career aspirations to game plans during change.

For example, Espinoza notes: "Everyone talks about pursuing your passion. Following your heart. Taking the right steps to land your "dream job". But what happens if your dream job NEVER shows up?" From there, she talks about the types of strategies that involve adopting a lifelong learning goal, learning to live with and grow in a 'sidetrack job', and re-envisioning a new 'dream job' goal.

The trap lies in old paradigms of happiness and achievement. As chapters probe old scenarios and new responses to adversity, readers learn some fundamentals for leading revised lives no matter what the misfortunes and new conditions dictate.

Nurturing yourself isn't about taking a bubble bath and forgetting it all. Nor is it about getting a massage or reading a good book. It involves the kind of self-care that comes through flexibility, adaptation, and the ability to field blows and use them to formulate new visions of a productive, happier life.

All these elements and more are surveyed in a practical guide that's highly recommended for libraries strong in education and career subjects, positive psychology, and new age thinking alike.

~ D. Donovan, Senior Reviewer, Midwest Book Review

Nurturing Our Self

During college, everyday life, and the job search

Lily E. Espinoza

Alive Book Publishing

Nurturing Our Self
During college, everyday life, and the job search
Copyright © 2022 by Lily E. Espinoza

All rights reserved. No part of this book may be reproduced or transmitted in any form or by any means without written permission from the publisher and author. Additional copies may be ordered from the publisher for educational, business, promotional or premium use. For information, contact ALIVE Book Publishing at: alivebookpublishing.com, or call (925) 837-7303.

Book Design by Alex Johnson; Front cover art by Yuri Morita
Back cover art by Sarah

Figure 1, Page 55, Credit: Institute of Medicine. 1994.
Reducing Risks for Mental Disorders: Frontiers for Preventive Intervention Research. https://doi.org/10.17226/2139.
Reproduced with permission from the National Academy of Sciences, Courtesy of the National Academies Press, Washington, D.C.

ISBN 13
978-1-63132-164-1

Library of Congress Control Number: 2022907541
Cataloging-in-Publication Data is available upon request.

First Edition

Published in the United States of America by ALIVE Book Publishing
an imprint of Advanced Publishing LLC
3200 A Danville Blvd., Suite 204, Alamo, California 94507
alivebookpublishing.com

PRINTED IN THE UNITED STATES OF AMERICA

10 9 8 7 6 5 4 3 2 1

Table of Contents

Foreword	9
Acknowledgements	13
Preface	15
Introduction	21

Part I – Nurturing Our Self During College 37

College Nurturing Overview	39
Literature Review	45
College Student Health Evolution	49
Health in the Modern Era	53
Assessing Healthy Practices on the College Campus	59
Well-being Practices on the College Campus	63
The Nurturing Framework on the College Campus	67
Creating the Nurturing Framework Model	69
Student Facing and Institution Facing Support Using the Nurturing Framework	73
A Course Outline Using the Nurturing Framework	75
Mind Unit	75
Embodiment Unit	76
Spiritual Unit	76
Community Unit	77
Policy Based on the Nurturing Framework	79
Campus Community Development Based on the Nurturing Framework Model	81
Summary	83

Part II - Nurturing Our Self in Everyday Life   85

Sleep	87
Effective Mind Body Medicine Treatments	88
Sleep Health Education and Practices	89
Learning About Sleep for Students	90
Personal Dignity	91
Stress Reduction and the Type A personality	95
What is the Type A Personality?	95
Characteristics of the Type A Personality	95
What Are the Health Risks of a Type A Personality?	96
Why Don't Type A People Just Relax?	96
When the Type A Personality Goes Overboard	96
Stress relief with coursework	97
Stress relief in everyday life	97
Stress relief in the community	98
Physical Activity	99
My Father's Experience of Gratitude	101
Everyday Health on the College Campus	109
Social and Personal Support Programs	111
Institutional Support Programs	111
Academic Programs in Health and Well-being	112
Healthy Behavior Change	113

Part III - Nurturing Our Self During the Job Search   117

Rugged Individualism is a Myth	119
Personal Bias Can be Transcended	121
Life Transitions are Times of Community Nurturing	125
Getting Sidetracked is Par for the Course	129
Look Back and Forward in Gratitude	133
Prove Yourself Even in the Small Roles	135

Passion Projects Rock	139
Making Space for Professional Loyalty	143
Road House Rules	147
Nope, Enough Ain't Enough	151
Snowball's Chance in Hell	155
The Joy of Staying Busy When You Are Unemployed	159
Being Excellent While Unemployed	167
Patience is a Bear	169
When the Star Player is Benched	173
The F Word - Feedback	175
The Power of the Forces of Good and Evil	177
Taking a Career Pause	181
Loving Thoughts on Being a College Intern	183
HRMS Blues	187
Diversity, Equity & Inclusion for the New Generation	191
Career Advancement in Student Services	195
Achieving Inner Peace	201
Getting Your Foot in the Door in Higher Education	207
One Truly Unfortunate Interview	213
Wowing the Crowd for Your Interview Presentation	217
Mentors are Immortal	221
Getting Your First Full-time Job in Student Services	225
Positivity Starts Inside Our Self	231
Perceiving Strength in Others	235
Making Positive Decisions as a Manager	237
Nurturing the Body Politic	243
We are in a Time of Metamorphosis	249
References	253
Online Resources	261
About the Author	263

Foreword

August 2017, there I was one night, sitting in my first graduate course at John F. Kennedy University in Pleasant Hill, CA thinking, "What the hell have I gotten myself into?" Here I am in my forties and I decided to start a new chapter in my life. I was working full time and commuting for work to and from downtown San Francisco every day; now, I was adding one more thing to my plate. "Well," I thought, "Here goes nothing." A few minutes go by, and it's just the professor and me. I think to myself, "Well, this is awkward. I hope the other students come in." Another couple of minutes go by and in walks another student, who later I find out to be Lily; Whew! I am not the only one in this class. The professor tells us another student is enrolled but he will not be in that evening, it was just Lily and me. The following week, the other student arrived, and we nicknamed ourselves The Big Three (since it was just the three of us in the class). We three made a promise to look out for one another. We began with introductions. I can't remember who went first, but after Lily introduced herself, I remember thinking, "Damn, this woman has accomplished a lot!" By the time Lily and I met, she had already completed a Doctorate, a Master's, had a successful career, AND published her first book, *Not Getting Stuck (Alive Publishing, 2017)*. I thought to myself, 'She's about to be my new grad school best friend!'

At the beginning of our first semester of grad school, we were determined, and we all agreed that failure was not an option, no matter how difficult the course. So, let me digress and say, if you are taking that next step in your graduate school program, find yourself a partner in crime, like Lily. Without her and the third partner of the Big Three, I could not have completed the program without them.

During those first few class meetings, we talked a little more about the program we were in (Master of Arts degree in Health Education) and what we wanted to get out of the program. The health program we were in looked at Holistic Health Education through a holistic lens. What is holistic health? Holistic health focuses on the whole person: physical, mental, emotional, social, intellectual, and spiritual.

The following two years were not only the longest years of our lives, but they were also a blur. One minute we are trying to figure out what assignment is due that week. The next minute, we are presenting our capstone projects and graduating. During those two years, we worked tirelessly on our capstone projects. We presented our projects to current and former students at the university.

My own project consisted of creating a breastfeeding program designed for African-American women. While completing my course work, I was a Family Health Advocate at San Francisco Black Infant Health. SF Black Infant Health provided African-American pregnant women with prenatal and postpartum sessions. In addition, these groups give Black women an opportunity to be in community with one another. A true community health program, *the Black Infant Health (BIH) Program aims to improve health among African American mothers and babies. BIH reduces the Black/White disparities by empowering pregnant and mothering African American women to make healthy choices for themselves, their families, and their communities.*

To address college student stress, Lily's capstone project consisted of a Nurturing Framework Course geared toward students entering college. This framework is the foundation for a well-being course based on a 11-week term and a curriculum outline that is divided into four units. What was unique about Lily's project was how useful and necessary it is for college students. As Lily writes in her book, "a third of students have experienced emotional turmoil that affected their college participation." As a result, students experience high levels of stress and anxiety- both mentally and physically, sleeplessness, loneliness, isolation, etc.- as they navigate the college experience. Thinking back to my own college experience, I also experienced high stress and anxiety as I transferred from a junior college to a university. Had I known about a book like Lily's, I might have done a better job at managing my stress and anxiety.

I was extremely honored and thrilled that Lily asked me to write the foreword to her second book. I am incredibly proud that she took a theory and turned it into an idea that is featured in her book. What I love about *Nurturing Our Self: During College, Everyday Life, and the Job Search* is it is an excellent resource for those who work with college students or as educators in wellness programs.

Lily comes with a wealth of experience in the education field. She has been the Dean and director of several student support programs, has run departments and campus operations, and was a transfer student herself who personally went through the process. If I forgot to mention this before, Lily's first book, *Not Getting Stuck*, is based on conversations about Latina students experience as transfer students and she spoke candidly about her own experience transferring to a four-year university. With her personal and employment background along with her studies in the Master of Arts Holistic Health Education program, Lily has gained expertise in tapping into nurturing oneself throughout the different phases of our lives.

Well, I have done enough talking. It's now time for you all to take the time and nurture yourselves!

Michele D. Callwood
M.A Health Education
John F. Kennedy University
PBIS (Positive Behavior Intervention Supports) Coach
San Francisco Unified School District
February, 2022

Acknowledgements

This book would not be possible without the support of so many over the years. I am indebted to the kindness of humanity and to those who extended a helping hand. I include gratitude for those who no longer walk this earth. Praise for friendships that transcend space and time!

Let me start by thanking my dear friends Cathy and Efrain Jasso who opened their heart and home to me and my son, Justice, when I was faced with the potential of being homeless. Thank you to the Singh family for providing support and a sense of connection for my son to his heritage and culture.

My career path and my education path has always been interconnected. A big thanks for my friends in my graduate program in Holistic Health Education at John F. Kennedy University. Together we were known as the Big Three, Michele Callwood, and Thomas Hogan. Thanks to the JFK faculty in 2017-2019, Nina Fry-Kizler, Robin Heggum, Carole Henmi, and the unforgettable and incomparable, Professor Fall Ferguson. Also, I give gratitude to the faculty in higher education administration at Columbia University in the city of New York in 2001-2002, the beloved L. Lee Knefelkamp, Monica Christensen, Kevin Dougherty, and Gregory M. Anderson. From my time at California State University, Fullerton 2008-2011, I thank Professors Dawn Person, John Hoffman, and Ronni Sanlo. From Mills College, I thank Erica Dominguez. Also, I am thankful for the community college mentors, colleagues, and former supervisors I have worked with over time including the ornery Jean Thomas, Kenneth Meehan, Eloy Ortiz Oakley, Rajen Vurdien, Jowel Laguerre, Arturo Reyes, Erin Vines, Rosa Perez, Victoria Lugo, Alexis Montevirgen, Diane Scott-Summers, Nicola Place, Emily Stone, Bernadine

Chuck Fong, Martha Kanter, Leticia Delgado, Jerome Hunter, David Wain Coon, Peter Garcia, Newin Orante, Helen Benjamin, John Hernandez, Mike Muñoz, Shariq Ahmed, Eric Rabitoy, Huu Nguyen, Dana Hester, Tran Hong, David Poole, Martha McDonald, Earic Dixon-Peters, Carol Mattson, Ketmani Kouanchao, Juan Carlos Astorga, Cristy Passman, Karen Oeh, Janine Cirrito, Flor Aguilar, Chris Lam, John Abelon, Jane Ishibashi, Karyn Nguyen, Kris Kaiger, Kathleen O'Connell Hodge, Ann Hovey, Peter Fong, Paul McKinley, Ruth Sipple, and Larry Buckley. Thanks to those along the way that I met from various California communities, those from my hometown in Fullerton, CA and in Morningside Heights in New York City, Jamaica Plain in Boston, and friends from my many journeys around the San Francisco Bay Area. I would not have survived the tough days in 2014-2017, without the state of California public assistance I received - unemployment insurance, CalWORKs, CalFresh, MediCal, housing assistance, and job assistance though Goodwill Industries of the Greater East Bay, and the Workforce Development Board of Solano County. Believe it or not, I also appreciate all the cool customers I served while I worked as a Lyft driver and as a wine tour guide in the Napa Valley who helped me put food on the table for my family.

Mil gracias to my loving family including my son, Justice, my sisters Janet Needham, Wendy Espinoza Cotta, and my brother Lawrence Ploski. Most of all, I owe a debt of gratitude to my ancestors and my dearly departed mother Margarita Espinoza, dearly departed father Donald Ploski, and also in spirit, my grandparents, William and Mary Ploski, and Francisco Sanchez Espinoza and Isabella Marina Lugo. As well, I appreciate future generations of family who are in my thoughts of who are yet to come.

Preface

This book is my pandemic project. Covid-19 turned the world upside down in multiple and various ways. For me, I found myself unemployed, questioning global public health policies, and wondering about the next stage in my career. While I was involuntarily unemployed, I found myself swept up in the Great Resignation, which was happening everywhere in the year 2021. People across all sectors were re-evaluating their purpose and the meaning of work. Partly due to the strain from the on-going waves of Covid-19 infections and partly because the workplace is placing greater demands on workers with advancement in technology and outcome metrics, more workers than ever are seeking to strike a better balance between work and life as a direct result of the global pandemic. With the rising costs of living for basic needs like housing, transportation, childcare and rapid inflation, many people are questioning the real value of work.

When I lost my job in August 2020, it was five months after the state of California went into full lockdown in response to Covid-19. For five months, I pivoted my role to work 100% remote and my son pivoted to remote schooling. After pivoting all my work to remote, I got that dreaded call that my employment was terminated. In years past, whenever I had been fired, I would have done a 360 degree evaluation of my personal skills, abilities, and behaviors that led to the unfortunate experience. But this time I was fired during a global pandemic. I would not have access to the same resources I had used in years past to find a new position. I was facing a total uncertainty about my future for me and my family. Giving myself a pandemic project helped me to stay focused.

This book is a collection of academic work and reflections of my career path as a professional involved in higher education for over 20 years. The research is based on my Master of Arts degree in Holistic Health Education from John F. Kennedy University which I completed in 2019. The irony is that the reason I returned to graduate school back in 2017 was as a response to getting fired in 2014, and being unemployed for 3 years. Back in 2014, my employment contract had ended without renewal, so I planned to pivot my career from working in higher education to working in what might be a health-related career. As I would later come to find out, every career is a health-related career.

The book has three distinct, disparate parts. In the first part, I present the Nurturing Framework Model based on holistic health education research and analysis using the lens of student development theory. This model can be used to help college students deal with stress in college and after they graduate, who are often underprepared to enter the workforce. After the research, there is a section based on personal reflections that explore my experience of losing a career working in the field of higher education. I had always believed in the quote, "If you do what you love, you'll never work a day in your life." For most of my career, I felt like I was doing what I loved, so when I lost my job in 2014, I found myself both brokenhearted and out of work. I needed to make myself whole, my mind, body, spirit, and my sense of community. I began cataloging my job search in 2014 and the reflections in this book represent the time from being unemployed in 2014 to 2020, to when the pandemic began. During that time, I also became a contributor to a wellness health magazine, so included in this book is a section of articles from the online magazine site. One special inclusion in this book is an article I found from my father from 1961. My dad's article describes a motorcycle adventure in Japan that made him reflect on gratitude. My father, who passed away in 2004, was a brilliant writer, so I am honored to have found a piece of his writing that aligns with the theme of this book which is about well-being. While the world has started to slowly open back up thanks to the Covid-19 vaccines, this book represents a mixture of love, gratitude, and hope for a future with the notion of nurturing baked in.

Lily E. Espinoza
Benicia, CA
2022

Life Well Lived

A life well lived is a precious gift
Of hope and strength and grace,
From someone who has made our world
A brighter, better place
It's filled with moments, sweet and sad
With smiles and sometimes tears,
With friendships formed and good times shared
And laughter through the years.
A life well lived is a legacy
Of joy and pride and pleasure,
A living, lasting memory
Our grateful hearts will treasure

- Author Unknown

Introduction

Sitting in a local bar called Good Life got me thinking about life. The Good Life had turned into a regular hangout for me. My friends and I were there when it first opened its doors on Massachusetts Avenue in Cambridge, and we became regulars on Friday evenings. I was kinda recreating my own Cheers fantasy from the 1980's television show, being that we were right across the Charles River in Boston where the Cheers bar is located. That one night I wondered, "Had I "made it" in life? Was this really the Good Life?"

I was 25 years old. It was the year 2000 (Y2K) and I was a recent college graduate, having just completed my Bachelor of Arts degree just two years prior. I was working at Harvard University. Hanging out with friends drinking martinis at Good Life on a Friday evening. The late summer sun was bright and there was a jazz band playing beautiful music that fit the ambience perfectly. But suddenly, the place felt so empty and meaningless. What was I doing with my life? Was this really the Good Life? Is this all there is? It seemed like I was not doing enough with my life.

Now that I have a better perspective on life, I realize that in fact, I was having a quarter-life crisis. I had overcome insurmountable obstacles to reach that point in my life, but as I stood on that plateau of my life's journey at the ripe age of 25 years, I was left feeling unsatisfied. The quality of my life was not what I had wanted or hoped it to be. While I was working full-time, it did not feel like I was on the right career path. Something needed to change. I always believed that time waits for no one. In that moment, I felt I had no time to lose. I needed to make a change.

I was impatient with my life because I sensed my own

mortality in a very real way. My mother passed away in the year 1987, at the tender age of 37 years old due to breast cancer. I was 12 years old at the time. One of the outcomes of losing my mom at such as early age is that I swore to myself that I would live life to its fullest. Another outcome of losing my mother so young, and one many people who lose a parent early in life tend to have, is, I had developed a shortened lifespan expectation as part of my personal narrative. I figured I would probably die young, just like my mother. Hence, there I was, 25 years old worried I was running out of time. Feeling disappointed in myself because I was not living life to the fullest. I felt like I was letting myself down. I felt like I was wasting the precious little time I had on earth.

Because of the early loss of my mother, I have always been achievement oriented. While I was not even remotely academically gifted when I was young, I took advantage of extra-curricular activities during school. I was a thoroughly mediocre student in primary and secondary school, yet I was eager to participate in every afterschool activity I could. If only to travel to other schools as part of the sports team or for school band competitions. In my mind I was seeing the world! I was active in student government, drama productions, drill team, jazz band, marching band, volleyball, basketball, and the swim team. I was a below average student, but I got on every travel team I could find. I even tried out to be a varsity cheerleader. My senior year in high school, my subpar grades caught up with me. I dropped out of the varsity cheer tryouts because I did not meet the 2.0 GPA minimum eligibility to cheer. Oh, the irony! I was too dumb to be a cheerleader! Let that one sink in for a moment. I should not have been so surprised; my pathetic grade point average was also the reason I got booted out of student government my junior year. All through high school, I ditched classes so many times, I was required to attend night school to earn enough credits to graduate. After high school, the only higher education option for me was the community college route. At that point in my life, I felt like a complete and utter failure.

Not being one to take the easy way out, I decided to attend a community college 400 miles from my Orange County hometown in Fullerton, CA and moved to Pleasant Hill, CA in the east bay of the San Francisco Bay Area. Fortunately, I had an academic awakening in community college and opened my eyes to my full potential. Part of my awakening I credited to my discovering Women's Studies, a subject that challenged my prior assumptions and helpful college staff and faculty members who encouraged me to see myself as college material. Through hard work and many ups and downs, I managed to successfully transfer from the community college to a four-year university. I felt like I had completely redeemed myself. Now my life was going somewhere!

I transferred to the University of California, Berkeley and graduated with a Bachelor of Arts degree in Women's Studies. Even more important than the college degree, I had found my calling. My success at Berkeley convinced me that I had found my true sense of purpose, working at a community college to help other students who were just like me (low income, non-English speaking immigrant parent, marginalized and from an unstable household), to transfer to their dream school. I wasn't sure how and in what way, but I knew I wanted to work in the community college system. I saw community colleges as the dream makers of the higher education system. I wanted to help make higher education dreams come true for others.

After I graduated from University of California, Berkeley in 1998, I got a job working at a tech startup company, working on career assessment software program development. Day after day, I completed quality assurance on this career assessment program that was designed to help people find their future career path. The software program consisted of an assessment test, interpretation, and links to college programs to point people in the direction of training programs for various industries. When I completed the assessment based on my own interests, the program identified higher education administration as my career path and listed two schools in New York City that offered the major for higher education administration, Columbia University and New York University. I was truly interested in this career path, but I had no idea how I was going to make it all happen. I put the thought in the back of my mind.

One day, the owners of the company took all the staff to a fancy sushi lunch. I was young and naïve. I vividly recall the embarrassment I felt that day because I had never eaten at a fancy sushi restaurant before. I ignorantly asked for a spoon for my miso soup. I did not realize at the time that miso soup comes in a small bowl so that patrons could lift the bowl to their mouth to sip the soup. Little did I know but my minor embarrassment was nothing compared to the shocking news that was to come next. The bosses of my company waited to the end of lunch and then they informed us all it was to be our last day working at the company. The start-up had failed and was shutting down. It was completely bankrupt.

It so happened that around the same time, I had ended a long-term personal relationship. Seeing as I was now out of work and free as a bird, I took this chance to give myself a fresh start. I pivoted my life and got to planning to move to Boston. I packed all my earthly possessions into my 1990 Honda Civic and drove from the San Francisco Bay Area to Boston, MA to live with my sister. With no cell phone, no maps, and no idea how long the journey would take me, I drove by myself to Boston following directions I printed out from Mapquest.com, following interstate 80 east for 4 days and nights across the continent of the United States at the age of 23.

Once on the east coast, I went to work at various temp agencies working at some of the top finance firms in Boston, like Wellington Management, and Citizens Bank. After working as a temp in the financial sector, I landed a job working in the Budget Office of WGBH Educational Foundation in Boston. Every day I would eat lunch across the street at the Harvard Business School. One day it occurred to me that I should look for a job at Harvard University. I applied for every job I considered myself even remotely qualified. The day I got a call for an interview at Harvard University, I knew I was following my destiny. I knew if I got a job there, I would be one step closer to really making a difference for others. I showed up for the interview in a beautiful historic brick building in Harvard Square. I got the whole tour. I was offered the job! Believe it or not, I turned it down.

The position that I was offered was to work in the Annual Giving department in University Development. I did not see myself making calls to donors for annual gifts and inputting data entry for gift transactions. At first, I could not believe I made such a gutsy move. I turned down Harvard University! But I had to go with my instinct. It did not feel right. The surprising part was that the human resources manager called me shortly after I declined the job offer to discuss my application. She said she wanted to find a fit for me at Harvard University. She went out of her way to listen and understood what kind of position would best suit my skillset and my abilities, which were mainly in finance at that time.

Eventually, I found a position working in Planned Giving working with alumni wanting to arrange bequests and establishing annuities and trusts for the university. I was to be a coordinator of planned gifts which mainly consisted of processing stocks, property, bonds, and other financial holdings for donation to the university. I would spend my days hearing wonderful and amazing stories from alumni who were leaving huge sums of money to Harvard University. The lovely memories of college life only cemented the belief that I had held from my time in community college at Diablo Valley College, which is that the college experience is truly a life changing event. When a person goes to college, it not only changes the person for the better, but the world for the better, too!

Another interesting tidbit of information that I learned while working at Harvard University is that Harvard alumni have a different life expectancy than the average U.S. population. In fact, the department in which I worked in at Harvard uses an actuarial table that was specifically developed for Harvard alums to determine the payout amount for annuities and trusts. Another benefit of college beyond the learning, friendships, contributions to knowledge, and experience, attending college can literally extend your life expectancy! This realization made me believe, that everybody, from all walks of life, truly deserved the chance to go to college.

While working at Harvard University, I attended a few classes, because I was considering graduate school as a next step in my career. Also, I had a natural curiosity about what made Harvard so special. Part of the benefits of working at the university, I could receive tuition reimbursement. That meant I could attend graduate school on Harvard's dime. Not bad!

Yet, it was during this time, when I had my mid-life crisis sitting in Good Life that summer night. What was I doing with my life path? Something felt off. I did not see myself as a Harvard girl. I was torn about leaving Harvard University. The job was challenging but fun, and my co-workers were awesome! I had been living in Boston for two years. For the first time, if felt like I was truly happy and having the time of my life. But life was almost too good. My life felt so boring. Where was the challenge, the struggle? It was the end of the millennium and people sensed there was new energy coming our way, like the turning over of a new leaf. In the summer, I would rollerblade to the Hatch Shell to hear great free concerts. I had gone to Lilith Fair that summer and found the live music scene at hot spots around Boston. I lived in this amazing mansion on Jamaica Pond in

Jamaica Plain, a fun, colorful neighborhood with quirky shops and a fantastic Cuban restaurant steps from my front door. But something was telling me to leave. My time in Boston was coming to an end. Why would I leave all this behind?

I knew in my heart that I was not doing what I knew I was meant to be doing, which was working at a community college to help students who were like myself, low income, first generation, and marginalized within higher education. I combed over job opportunities at Harvard University. I incorrectly thought perhaps there might be a chance to get a position working in student services, but all the jobs required an advanced degree and experience working with college students. I had neither of those two requirements. I felt stymied.

I decided to begin applying to graduate schools in New York City. I applied to two schools, New York University and Columbia University. They were the same schools that were selected for me years ago when I was working at that tech start up from years before. The pièce de résistance, the programs I applied to had a built-in internship component that would provide me with direct experience working with students while I studied student development. Miracle of all miracles I was admitted to both schools. Not bad for a near high school drop-out from a broken home. I was admitted to both programs and decided to attend Columbia University, to get an ivy-league education. I could not believe that I got admitted to an ivy-league institution. I seriously impressed myself with that one!

I moved to New York City in August 2001. I was enrolled in the Student Personnel Administration Master of Arts program at Columbia University. It was a one-year program. I was placed in an internship working for Banc of America Securities in University Relations. My internship consisted of printing out resumes and sending the resumes to the human resources department for MBA graduates to get work in investment banking and securities for Banc of America Securities. I was living in

New York City working for a global financial institution, one month before the September 11 attacks, one of the worst terrorist attacks on American soil.

When a cataclysmic event happens, you question everything. On the morning of the terrorist attack, after watching the towers fall on television, I questioned my life course. I was stuck on the island of Manhattan wondering if this was going to be the place where I died. Did I make the biggest mistake of my life by leaving Boston? Was I supposed to leave? What was New York City and the world telling me in that moment? What was my life plan now? What did it all mean?

I remember the morning of September 11, I was working at the Solow Building at 9 West 57th Street in New York City. It was a sunny, bright, perfectly clear blue sky Tuesday. After the two planes flew into the World Trade Center towers and the towers fell, the city of New York was totally shut down. The city shut down the subways, the bridges were closed, no taxis were available, and it was total chaos. I walked from West 57th Street to my apartment on West 116th Street. I remember I decided to walk through Central Park so if another building was attacked, the building would not fall on me. During the 3.5 mile walk home, I was constantly looking up to the cerulean sky to see if any more planes were coming. There were no classes that night. I spent the day and night watching the news with my roommates who were also graduate students. There were no working phone lines and no internet. We were totally cut off from the world.

The next day I had a class at Columbia University on campus. For some reason, it did not occur to me that class might be cancelled. The phone lines were not working, and I had no laptop or computer. This was before the smart phone was invented. There was no way to know where to go or what to do. So, I walked to class on September 12 across the park to Amsterdam Avenue from Morningside Heights. That night I had class with

Prof. Gregory Anderson. It was in that class that I realized that I was in exactly the right place at the exact right moment in history for exactly what I needed to do with the rest of my life. I was not going anywhere. I was in the right place at the perfectly right time. I was 100% certain I had discovered my destiny. I had found my true career path!

The morning of September 11 changed everything, and it impacted my career and life choices in significant ways. It changed the way I saw myself, my career, my potential, and my purpose. It made me think deeply about my impact on the world and the systems that I am a part of and the impact of systems in the world around me. The systems that I was most concerned with were the systems of higher education. Here I was a product of the community college system. Because of that positive experience I was able to parlay that experience to be able to attend the best baccalaureate granting public institution of higher education in the world. Because of that experience I was able to parlay that into a full-time position working at the best private institution of higher education in the world. Because of that experience I was able to get admitted to a graduate program at the top institution for higher education administration in the world. With this new found appreciation of world systems, I felt this sense of urgency to build a more compassionate community, so all could have access to make a positive impact on the systems in the world. I felt compelled to give back and to work to open the doors for those behind me to make more positive impacts on the world in order to prevent events like September 11 from happening in the future! It was all so clear!

With a passion renewed and a purpose defined, I set out into the world the day after September 12. I took the bull by the horns. The first thing I did was quit my internship. I was not going to waste my one internship experience on working for Bank of America Securities. The financial system in the US is a major part of the problem, not a part of the solution to global politics! A few weeks later, I applied and accepted an internship at a STEM college preparation program at the Columbia University College of Physicians and Surgeons working with students of color from inner-city high schools. It was one of the best decisions of my life. That one decision helped me catapult myself into a lifelong career in education serving students and the community with compassion.

With over 20 years of experience, I now believe that our colleges must do everything in their collective power to support students' sense of purpose which starts with providing a nurturing environment. For eons, the purpose of higher education has been questioned and re-defined. What is the proper role of higher education as a social institution? Are college degrees for developing the workforce or for producing new knowledge? In my doctoral research I explored the reason students chose to attend college. Many students attend college for economic and sociological reasons, but it all comes down to the pursuit of living a good life. Everyone wants to live a life well-lived. And why not? That is a basic human need. Every person deserves the chance to live their life to the fullest.

Right now, the traditional American college experience is facing an existential threat with the ongoing crises over rising costs of living, social unrest, mental health, and physical health concerns with the Covid-19 pandemic and shifts in labor market demands. In addition, hiring practices and employer demands have shifted gears away from requiring college degrees as industries have transformed with automation, remote work, and changing demands of workers after the Great Resignation of 2021. In addition, there is the Silver Tsunamis as Baby Boomers leave the workforce in droves taking their historical knowledge with them. While companies are relying less on college degrees for the next generation in the workforce, lifelong learning has never been more important. Many traditional workers are pivoting careers and learning through micro credentials, technology boot camps, executive training, career coaching, digital badges, professional certification, competency-based learning, and skills-based hiring that highlight the importance of upskilling and keeping current with trends in hiring. The world of work is in a state of flux. It begs the question; will college campuses bend to the needs of the future workforce or will they remain relics of the past?

The social mystique and meaning behind higher education have held my curiosity over these many years entirely due to the ambiguous nature of the college experience. For some people, going to college is a life altering experience, yet for others it is a time of non-stop parties that hardly makes a dent in their life path. Many of the elderly Harvard alums I worked with were in the late stages of their life in their 70's 80's and 90's and their years at Harvard were the high point of their lives. I truly believe it is our duty and responsibility as college educators to turn our institutions of higher education into compassionate institutions that elevate the meaning of what it means to be human and the human condition.

For this reason, I believe it is the responsibility of higher education to look at the process of developing whole graduates that must drive higher education in a post-pandemic world and into the future. With everything that is now known about the brain, epigenetics, neuroplasticity, psychoneuroimmunology, neuroscience, biosocial development, learning, and human development, there is a duty to respond accordingly.

Recently, I was listening to a podcast, Remarkable People, by Guy Kawasaki who was interviewing Marc Benioff, CEO of Salesforce and owner of Time magazine and a multimillionaire many times over. Guy hired Marc as an intern at Apple in 1985. Marc was discussing his 1-1-1 concept of his philanthropy which equates to Marc donating 1% of the Salesforce company equity, product, and time in perpetuity. The 1-1-1 concept is about including the planet as a stakeholder. Marc called it stakeholder capitalism, redefining corporate citizenship to include not just by the development of great products but the inherent responsibility of all to help the planet, and a shared duty to integrate the company with the local community. A point of pride for Marc is that Salesforce employees volunteered over 6.5 million hours to community organizations. Marc discussed the Hawaiian concept of *Kuleana* which is about the role of responsibility. The deep sense of responsibility that covers a reciprocal relationship between the person who is responsible and the thing that they are responsible for. This beautiful philosophy proves the potential role of business to make a positive impact on the world. The system of higher education must take greater responsibility for the students' well-being and the world in which the students will live.

Also, there is the Native American saying that says "the test of good planning is in what it succeeds in doing." Our college campuses must be sites where nurturing happens in order to graduate whole students who have purpose, meaning, and passion to support adults to live a life well-lived. I see future college campuses as charging stations for people to fill up on skills, learning, and positive behaviors and attitude to handle the stress of living in a post-pandemic world.

Another result of starting my career in the shadow of the 9/11 terrorist attack, is that I have held a fascination with emergency management and leadership during crisis incidents. I listen to another weekly podcast on the topic of emergency management where they talk about the four phases of emergency management - mitigation, preparedness, response, and recovery. I argue that there is a fifth stage in emergency management, regeneration. The world is in a state of regeneration as a by-product of the Covid-19 pandemic emergency and institutions of higher education must play their part in helping the world recover and regenerate for when the pandemic is over. As well, the workforce is in crisis in conjunction with the on-going climate crisis and higher education has a responsibility to regenerate our college missions to consider our future workforce and the environment as equal constituencies.

As a lifelong student of leadership, I am also curious about how leaders face challenges. Within leadership circles there are two terms that describe challenges, VUCA and BANI. VUCA is volatility, uncertainty, complexity, ambiguity. BANI is brittle, anxious, nonlinear, and incomprehensible. By using the terms VUCA and BANI, leaders can determine various approaches from which to solve challenges. The problem with our current situation of the environment in 2022, is that it will take a holistic and integrative approach to become whole after the shift that has recently taken place. Yet higher education continues to act competitively rather than collaboratively. Even at Harvard, they have a favorite saying, every tub on its own bottom. Basically that translates to every man for himself. The world is small, and our changing environment means we must consider relationships and interconnections like never before. Our decisions must be based on compassion and nurturing to move forward with inclusion and equity for all. Learning about VUCA and BANI provides educators with tools to develop approaches to handle challenges that appear insurmountable.

Conquering the insurmountable has been ongoing along my own life journey. In this journey of learning my true passion and my purpose in life, I have attempted to put to paper a few ideas that can help those currently working with college students, tips for everyday life, and lessons learned as an educator on the job search. This book is a culmination of many hours of reflection as a college educator. The book is divided into three parts to aid educator planners, students, and community leaders to see a path forward after the pandemic.

Part One of the book is where I introduce the Nurturing Framework for working with college students and on the college campus for students, faculty, and staff to develop resiliency.

Many college students believe a college degree is all you need to get a ticket to Easy Street. Unfortunately, I have learned that is simply not the case. A college degree is no guarantee against unemployment and hardship later in life. For many low income and students of color, a college degree may close more doors that it opens, because of college debt and systematic racism and sexism, as I personally experienced. The research I present is a compilation of my work as a graduate student in the Master of Arts degree program at John F. Kennedy University in Pleasant Hill, CA. I completed this holistic graduate program after completing my Associate of Arts degree, Bachelor of Arts degree, Master of Arts degree, and doctoral degree, so the work is informed by my lived experience and advanced perspective after a career working with students from all walks of life. The introduction of the Nurturing Framework is critical at a time when there is political discourse about the "hardening" of schools and public education. As well it is informed by the educator activists of Critical Race Theory and the works of educators and philosophies on diversity, equity, inclusion, and accessibility including anti-racism practices with the intention of establishing praxis to build community and belonging for all.

In Part Two, there are articles that demonstrate how to incorporate nurturing ways during our everyday lived experience that strengthen our self and our communities. As adults, we work day in and day out with our mind on auto pilot. It is all too easy to lose sight of the value of a good night's sleep or appreciation for the dignity of our children and the process of making healthy behavior changes. Slowing down our thought patterns with new awareness and consciousness to re-examine our own assumptions and predispositions to better understand our own core beliefs and values are critical to nurturing our self every day. Many core beliefs that are established as an adult come from myths, misconceptions, and false information that can be detrimental to our health and everyday lives. Fortunately, being in relation with our self in a nurturing way provides space for us to parent ourselves in a healthy way to undo the damage of negative thoughts and behaviors. The path to nurturing the self begins with self-knowledge.

In the final section of the book is Part Three, the most personal in nature and blog-style in format. There is a collection of thoughts and reflections of lessons learned after facing some of life's most difficult moments, as well as some humorous antidotes and observations. Included are reflections on losing my dream job, facing unemployment, going through the loss of loved ones and mentors, questioning my career path, completing college interviews, switching career paths, trying out side hustles and the gig economy, opening my own consulting business, and general reflections about being an educator with years of experience at two-year colleges, four-year colleges, graduate schools, and public and private universities.

Nurturing our self is more than self-care. It is about knowing our self, listening to our self, and taking care to consciously be true to our self. Since an early age, I have been looking for clues, signs, symbols, meaning, and messages to lead me in the right direction for my life so that I could say I lived a well-lived life. I was overly concerned with wasting time and conscious of mortality as a constant threat. Once I slowed way, way down and learned to listen to my mind, body, spirit, and my community, it became clear that what I needed to do was to feel nurtured. Take this time to nurture yourself, your mind, body, spirit, and your community. Our world, as we know it, depends on it. Here's to wishing all of us, the Good Life!

Part I

Nurturing Our Self During College

1

College Nurturing Overview

Alma mater /älmə'mädər/ noun. Kind and nourishing mother or the school, college, or university that one once attended.

Nurture /'nərCHər/ verb. The process of caring and encouraging the growth or development of someone or something.

For many students, going off to college can feel like travelling to the Land of Oz. It can be so easy to get lost in the exhilaration of being on the other side of the rainbow that they lose sight of their sense of self and their oneness. It is no coincidence that the college years and the early 20's are when many people experience an identity crisis.

Especially for students of color, first generation college students, and students from underrepresented groups like LGBTQIA+ students, students with learning/physical/mental disabilities, and military veterans, college can be a time of uncertainty and trying to fit in and belong. There is even greater pressure than ever with the Covid-19 pandemic, rising cost of higher education, uncontrolled gun violence, ongoing racial tensions, and increased awareness of sexual assault with the #MeToo movement. For this reason, there is a major mental health crisis on college campuses across the United States.

Fortunately, advances in health promotion and the growing interest in student well-being and belonging are poised to take center stage. College campuses, professional student services staff, and strategic planning efforts have been slowly making the change to implement a holistic perspective when it comes to student support. For the first time, major research and funding are following the need to address mental health crises to support student well-being head-on, so to speak.

This book provides a way forward using the Nurturing Framework (NF) for stress reduction and overall student well-being and belonging in higher education that addresses the classroom, the campus, and college standards of practice.

Part I of this book provides an overview of how to institute nurturing on the college campus. There is an explanation for the sense of urgency and the importance of using the holistic approach for overall academic and personal college student well-being.

Next, there is an explanation of the importance of holistic grounding of the research. That holistic grounding is the evidence-based foundation for the development of the Nurturing Framework presented here for the first time. It is my contention that the discussion around college student well-being has been limited in scope over the last century.

Though there are dozens of models of student development in place since the field began over 100 years ago, not many theories include the importance of nurturing and student well-being. In fact, the purpose of higher education has bounced and shifted from job training to knowledge production to global citizenship to critical thinking to applied technology.

This book presents the first known model on nurturing for higher education that provides an integrative approach to college student well-being. Using an approach that addresses the mind, body, soul, and community, the holistic approach in this book is a distinct perspective on addressing college student well-being.

Next to follow the discussion on the holistic ground is a review of the relevant literature on the topic of student well-being. This section includes a review of research areas of student health data, college student development, current understanding of health practices on the college campus and relevance of well-being in the college experience, and a critical examination of specific student support programs currently in practice on college campuses.

Following the literature review is the discussion of an evidence-based solution, the Nurturing Framework, which I developed to provide a holistic approach to optimize college student academic and personal achievement.

Lastly, there is a summary that provides a description of key concepts of the framework and recommendations for further research.

Living is All About Our Ability to Adapt to Change

Having over twenty years of experience working as a student services professional, my educational philosophy is greatly influenced by educational researchers and other social science theories about education. One controversial philosopher that has always piqued my imagination over the years is Henri Bergson (1859–1941) known as the father of the concept of *élan vital* (Ansell-Pearson and Schrift, 2014). *Élan vital* is the concept of this invisible driving force (like the Allspark from the Marvel Universe) for evolutionary changes in living organisms within complex systems. That concept cements the notion that all living organisms exist in a constant state of growth, adaptation, and change. This generative principle is what defines the state of being alive for all living creatures – we all have this innate drive to develop, change, grow, and make necessary desirable adaptations (Ansell-Pearson, K., & Schrift, A. D., 2014). From this foundation of the inevitability of change as a human condition, my interest in student development and social identity development evolved into fascination with student well-being.

Most of my career has been in the work of student services at institutions of higher education. One of the reasons I dedicated my career to this field is because of the tremendous amount of potential change that college students go through during the college experience. This period of going to college is an experience that has the potential to establish healthy lifelong habits and attitudes that can positively affect a student and those in the students' lives long after formal education ends.

Many people develop lifelong habits during their college years that can have lasting impacts not only on themselves but their families, communities, and even the whole world. The undergraduate experience is a window of opportunity to support the development of healthy habits of mind, body, soul, and community through student support programs and higher education policy.

Mind, Body, Spirit, and Community

Two theories are the underpinning for what I call the Nurturing Framework model. These theories provide a focus on health promotion in college that binds together concepts of student development and health promotion. The first theory is the Bronfenbrenner's social ecology model. The social ecology model is the theory of the quality and context of interrelatedness across personal and environmental factors from the individual to family to community and finally to the level of public policy development. This model is useful for the NF framework because I wanted to explore the connected relationship between the individual and community that influence the healthy habits of college students. College policies impact the individual student to personal relationships with others to the relationship with the school, and the community. Student and community interactions then lead to policies that affect the overall environment throughout the college experience. My hope and goals are to help professionals working with students gain a wider perspective of the importance of personal opportunities for growth and change in actions and behaviors within the relationships, connections, and structures student find themselves in as college students.

Some of the concepts in the social ecology model that are especially relevant are social connections and interrelatedness between the student and the environment. Students can build awareness and knowledge of their health, specifically their ability to improve their state of well-being, based on the choices they make to build and form in social connections and relationships with other students and within their environment. This work to develop the Nurturing Framework is dedicated to improving the learning environment through the lens of the college student as the one experiencing the college environment.

The second theory driving this research is the theory of salutogenesis. Salutogenesis, or the focus on the origins of health and factors that support well-being rather than placing focus on disease prevention, as the underlying concept that guides the content of the framework and the recommendations for practice (Antonovsky, 1987).

Many programs and services developed for college wellness programs are based on risk prevention. In fact, the most recent CAS standard is designed around this very topic called *Preventing High-Risk Behaviors and Building Healthy Campuses*. CAS is the acronym for the Council for the Advancement of Standards which is used for the development of service delivery and scope of programs, services, and professional development and new staff training in higher education. This most recently updated CAS standard is based on a cross-function collaboration with 41 member associations in higher education with over 115,000 professionals from around the world, focused on structural and policy level changes for preventing high-risk behaviors. CAS was formed in 1979 with a mission to work on fostering and enhancing student learning, development, and achievement in higher education. Topics included within the new CAS standard for healthy campuses are drinking cessation, smoking cessation, drug cessation, sexual violence prevention, and hazing, suicide, self-harm, anxiety, depression, loneliness, and disordered eating issues on college campuses (CAS, 2019). This focus on risk prevention does not address the concept of health promotion on the college campus. The new 2019 CAS standard leaves a gap in assessment, services, and programs for campus health promotion.

The theories of health promotion within the construct of salutogenesis provide a proper lens to identify evidence-based areas to support college student development, growth, change, and personal adaptations naturally taking place such as learned optimism, well-being, and social connectedness.

Students come to college during a time in their lives where there is tremendous potential for growth, change, and transformation. With that in consideration, the traditional learning environment for undergraduates was traditionally designed to develop habits of the mind. The mind or the intellect was the predominant area of focus for in and out of class curriculum planning and services. The traditional learning environment was centered on classroom instruction, academic tutoring, course or major selection, research support, and perhaps on occasion, career training.

Over the last 100 years within the field of student development, there has been more inclusion of psychosocial programs and services, but even so, there has not been a holistic approach that centered on the mind, body, spirit, and community connection in student services and across student programming. Most college campuses have Health Centers based on the medical model and risk prevention. Fortunately, in recent times college campuses have started to develop wellness programs and services in addition to general health education. The Nurturing Framework presented here is unique in that it focuses on social connections and relationships from the students' perspectives to be in natural alignment with students' own élan vital.

2

Literature Review

Even before the Covid-19 pandemic, college students had been experiencing health problems on college campuses at an alarming rate. According to the National College Health Assessment (NCHA) report for fall 2019, students identified the top four factors that impact their academic performance as the following:

Table 1: NCHA Factors Affecting Student Performance, Fall 2019

Factor	Overall student population
Stress	37.6%
Anxiety	27.6%
Sleep Disorders	22.1%
Depression	21.5%

These factors beat out other commonly recognized risk factors such as drinking (3.3%), physical/sexual assault (.8%), eating disorders (2.8%), and sexually transmitted diseases/infections (0.4%). The survey also asked students to identify any sources of violence on campus with verbal threat being the highest source of violence for 11.6% of male students and 8.9% of female students.

In terms of mental health, there is a high number of students experiencing mental health issues. Students reported that in the last 12 months they experienced the following:

Table 2: NCHA Mental Health Factors Affecting Performance by Gender

Mental Health Factor	Male Population	Female Population
Feeling Exhausted	73.5%	88.2%
Overwhelmed	76.7%	91.9%
Anxiety	45.6%	68.6%
Lonely	55.2%	68.4%
Depressed	31.6%	43.3%

While college is designed to challenge students to stretch their intellectual and academic abilities, it is not meant to be a place of mental exhaustion, stress, and anxiety. The NCHA survey (Fall 2019) results highlight the importance of providing supports and programs that strengthen health promotion to prevent and protect against these issues affecting undergraduates on the college campus.

On the surface, there is sufficient evidence to indicate student physical health has been an important part of college campuses since the beginning of the university system in the United States. Universities have a long history of being concerned with the health and welfare of the college students in their care (Thelin, 2004). As previously mentioned, the term *alma mater* translates from Latin to mean "kind and nourishing mother" or "nursing mother." The connotation is that the university provides intellectual nourishment or sustenance for the development of the mind. This intellectual nourishment has also been beneficial for society as well as the well-being of the body, soul, and community of the college student. Universities were viewed in decades past as a "pseudo-parent" of the student, the Latin term often used to describe colleges and universities was *in loco parentis*, which translates to acting in the place of the parent regarding the safe keeping of the student or acting in ways that would be in the best interest for the student. Just as the role of modern-day parents have changed over time, so too has the role of the university in undergraduate education. In fact, there have been many changes in the role of the university as well as the role of the student yet concern over student well-being and college public health issues have not only continued but it has grown from a passing interest to a major source of research, resource allocation, policy, and student health programming, strategic planning, and development.

3

College Student Health Evolution

The field of student development arose as an academic discipline to understand and explore college student intellectual growth and the impact of college on the college student (Pascarella & Terenzini, 1997). There is over 100 years of research on college student outcomes that include theories and models of behavior change in college. Colleges play a significant role in the impact on the development of student verbal, quantitative and subject matter competence. But just as importantly, there is empirical evidence of psychosocial changes, cognitive skills, and intellectual growth, as well as a change in the attitudes, values, and moral development of students. There is also evidence of the overall impact of college on students' educational attainment, persistence, career and economic impact, and quality of life after college. College attendance is a strong indicator for success not just for the college student but also for those in their immediate family, communities, and associations. In a study from 1991, there was evidence that "the net benefits of a college education are not restricted to the person who attends college but are passed along to off-spring" (p. 589, P&T, 1995). Clearly the intergenerational influence that college has on communities means that the college student experience has long lasting effects on society in general. Therefore, the alarming trends of the decline of overall health of college students should be a major concern for more than the college administrators themselves.

While college is a time of tremendous growth and development, the NCHA survey demonstrates that college students are experiencing stress and anxiety at such high levels that it interferes with their academic life. Within the college student development field, a popular model explains behavior (B) is a function (f) of environment (E) and psychology (P), represented in the following equation: $[B = f(P \times E)]$ (Lewin, 1936). Therefore, if students are experiencing stress and anxiety, there are two approaches to address the problem behavior: approach 1 is to address environmental factors and approach 2 is to address the psychological factors of the student.

Creating the ideal learning environment has been the goal for many colleges and universities since they first began (Strange & Banning, 2001). Many faculty members carefully design the learning environment of the curriculum, classroom, and administrators and student affairs professionals carefully design the learning environment of both in-class and out-of-class space. But often, the learning environment has not been considered under the guise of the holistic concerns of the mind, body, spirit, and community. For example, in residential colleges, often the dorms or sleeping quarters, have been considered the optimum setting for student development programming and learning (Schroeder, 1999). Yet, stress and anxiety happen because of a confluence of factors both personal and academic for college students.

With the combination of the Covid pandemic on top of increasing college costs, gun violence in society, uncertainty in world politics, and increasing climate changes, modern college life is rife with overwhelming realties facing our college students unlike any previous generation (Kegan, 1994). In addition, many times there may not even be a physical learning environment, as dozens of colleges are opting for online, or distance education course offerings that remove the physical presence of a physical learning environment altogether. The online learning environment presents its own set of challenges, dangers, and pitfalls as students and instructors create new online worlds for learning in the modern society. Defining and safeguarding the optimum environment for learning has become increasingly difficult.

To address the psychological factors of the student, college health centers are often designated as the site for providing support for the treatment of the health, well-being, and overall psychology of the student. One of the first health centers in the nation opened in 1893 in the state of Michigan at the then called-Michigan State College which later became Michigan State University (Michigan State University, 2019). It was a medical facility which primarily focused on medical care of the students through offering isolation and in-patient care to prevent the spread of diseases. Over the years, the health center evolved from patient isolation to providing preventative care as well as containment of infectious diseases. With the influx of military veteran students after World War II and the GI Bill, many health centers on campuses grew in terms of capacity. In the 1970's, college health centers changed with the times to provide mostly outpatient services. In the 1980's more changes brought more services, "ancillary programs were expanded and an emphasis on health education was added. Women's health, sports medicine and health education" were given greater emphasis on the college campus (Michigan State University, 2019). In the 1990's health centers began to form collaborations across campus as resources were pooled with other departments such as disability services, recreation services, residential life, and international student services. Recently, in the 2010's colleges have been offering "neighborhood style" clinics within residential and campus areas that are comprised of clinic services and programs. Even with the evolution of the college health center and its variety of services and locations on campus, traditional college health centers have mainly focused on the provision of medical services, not health promotion.

These medical services focus on the prevention and health education around risky college student behavior as described in the CAS standards. The standards include information for addressing issues such as binge drinking, drug use, sexual assault, eating disorders, suicide prevention, hazing/bullying, and self-harm (CAS, 2019). Many of the standards are generalized; therefore they do not have standards based on ethnicity, gender identity, sexuality, or other personal or cultural or social identity indicators. Unfortunately, social determinants continue to be critical to overall health and it is essential for all health promotion programs to include personal identity regarding health measures. Not one of the CAS standards for college campus addresses stress.

In the next section of this literature review, I will discuss the current practices of health centers on college campuses. There will be an exploration of current programs and current trends on campus to address student health.

4

Health in the Modern Era

The concept of health and the relationship with personal wellness and well-being is not something new or recent. Records of well-being practices go back to ancient times from Indian Ayurveda to ancient Chinese medicine, to ancient Rome and Greece (Stara & Charvat, 2015). There were traditional healthcare systems that "emphasized one's lifestyle – nutrition, physical activity, quality of sleep, moderation, ethical behavior, development of positive thoughts and emotions through prayer of meditation" (p. 4, Stara & Charvat). In the West, many theories looked at mental illness and possible ways to determine mental health. The most well-known theory on wellness is the concept of "High-Level Wellness" first introduced by Halbert Dunn. He coined the term in the 1950's during a radio lecture series in the Washington, DC area (Ames, 2009). The concept involves three components,

1. The movement in the direction forward and upward towards a higher potential of functioning
2. The idea of an open-ended and ever-expanding tomorrow with its challenge to live at a fuller potential
3. Integration of the whole being of the total individual – body, mind, and spirit – in the functioning process.

Along with the key three concepts are eight points of high-level wellness which include having an open mind, freedom of expression, adjusting one's viewpoints, serving others, giving freedom to others, and facing inconsistencies in our own thinking.

Underpinning these concepts of maintaining our well-being and living a good life is the belief that health should be about the positive. The meaning of true health is more than the "absence of disease" (Ames, 2009).

Before Covid-19 emerged, there was a tremendous shift in notions of health that began with the 1979 Surgeon General's report on Health Promotion and Disease Prevention. The report stated that "the health of the American people has never been better" (Ames, 2009). This was due to the spectacular reduction in reported cases of life-threatening infections and communicable diseases. The report found 75% of deaths were mainly due to preventable deaths or "lifestyle" deaths due to degenerative diseases and not from infectious diseases, as was previously the biggest threat to overall health. This health statement reflected the shift in medical practices as medical care went through a paradigm shift from focusing primarily on infectious and communicable diseases to focusing on degenerative diseases such as heart disease, stroke, and cancer. The medical establishment took the logical next step to support disease prevention and health promotion which mirrored the changing global perspective of human health (Stara & Charvat, 2015). Universities slowly but surely followed suit in their changing perspectives on health and well-being of students on campus (NASPA, 2005).

In 1986, the World Health Organization cemented this notion of health as an aspirational state in the Ottawa Charter for Health Promotion. The Ottawa Charter opened the entire world of health to others outside the heath sector to address the importance of well-being. The Charter encourages all sectors to aid in the achievement of well-being, "health is, therefore, seen as a resource of everyday life, not the objective of living. Health is a positive concept emphasizing social and personal resources, as well as physical capacities. Therefore, health promotion is not just the responsibility of the health sector but goes beyond healthy lifestyles to well-being" (p. 1, WHO).

Chapter 4 55

The charter also emphasized the connection between the self, the community and environmental factors that influence health. This charter was the first policy to confirm that health can be created and promoted using "caring, holism, and ecology" based strategies. The everyday world is the location for the promotion of healthy environments including where people "learn, work, play, and love." Health is not simply obtained in a doctor's office or a medical clinic. By expanding the promotion of health outside of the health sector, people all over the world can take up the charge to promote their own and their community's good health.

In 2006 the Institute of Medicine (IOM) developed a model to address the role of disease prevention in public health planning. This model included new initiatives designed to build and strengthen capacity using the continuum of care model. The IOM protractor is used to treat behavioral health problems such as substance abuse, mental illness, eating disorders, obesity, and other risky behavior.

Figure 1

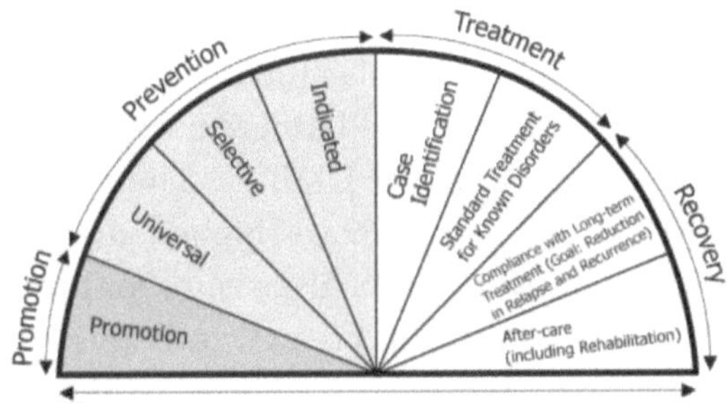

IOM Model of Continuum of Care

This model addressed other outdated ideas in the prevention, intervention, and treatment models that were faulty in serving various populations with distinct social and environmental issues. Whereas previous programs and services focused on the treatment and maintenance of illness, the current model includes the important area of prevention and more recently, health promotion. The concepts of *universal, selective,* and *indicated* helped to aid in developing services for specific populations. The extended categories now include population differences in the prevention of illness which considers social determinants of health. College campuses can develop public health preventions to address population level health promotion in a similar fashion.

Another area of interest is not only health promotion for undergraduate student well-being, but the role of healthy practices across the university for staff and faculty members as well. There is a rise in the significance of the concept of healthy universities in conjunction with the concern for student well-being both inside and outside the classroom.

The National Association of Student Personnel Administrators' (NASPA) Health Education and Leadership Program in 2005 proposed an ecological approach to "address health-related issues to achieve a healthy campus that is community-based and not just individually focused" (p. 3, NASPA). NASPA is the preeminent national association for college and university administrators. Health is recognized as the one variable that affects all students and plays a major role affecting academic performance. Healthy campuses affect not only student success but also student retention. In 2010, the United Kingdom reported success of student well-being projects. The UK has 2.3 million college students and 370,000 staff in the 169 UK higher education institutions. Especially because of national concerns for problems with obesity and other health-related issues, the Government committed to supporting healthy campus practices including developing "a strategy for health that integrates health into the organization's structure to create healthy working, learning, and living environments; increase the profile of health in teaching and research; and develop healthy alliances in the community." These health promotion projects showcase that not only is student and community well-being urgently needed for current health issues, but it offers assurance for future well-being and operational continuity. Dooris (2010) identified institutions of higher education as providing the "context that 'future shape' students and staff as they clarify values, grow intellectually and developed capabilities that can enhance current and future citizenship within families, communities, workplaces and society as a whole" (p.2, Dooris). The responsibility to shape society in healthy ways underscore the importance of having healthy college campuses for students as well as staff and college faculty.

5

Assessing Healthy Practices on the College Campus

In the United States, health promotion in higher education benefits from a history of assessment and quality assurance by the American College Health Association (ACHA). Assessment and quality assurance includes on-going additions to the body of knowledge and identifies scope of practice plus essential functions pertaining to the field. Since 1996 there have been three revisions to the Standards of Practice for Health Promotion in Higher Education (SPHPHE). The third edition in 2012, includes seven standards related to advocacy, education, and research. Health promotion standards list the following components:

1. Alignment with the Missions of Higher Education
2. Socioecological-based Practices
3. Collaborative Practice
4. Cultural Competency
5. Theory-based Practice
6. Evidence-informed Practice
7. Continuing Professional Development and Service

Using evidence, theory, and socioecological-based practices demonstrate the reach of higher education to motivate and transform lives for both the student and staff as well as the community and overall society.

Applying theory to practice is behind much of the work of the Bringing Theory to Practice project (BTtoP) (Love, 2013). More than 300 campuses worked together to develop theory and practices to document a "major initiative to affect greater understanding and comprehensive intentional action regarding the connections between intensive and engaging learning opportunities, civic development, and the well-being of students as whole persons" (p. 2). Colleges are an environment that can lead to positive social change through quality-based practices. These projects included topics such as the connection between civic engagement and well-being, connecting resources, academic and student life and civic centers for the common good and the importance of building "programs for which student well-being was the focus and reason for acting" (p. 4). These BTtoP projects harken back to the origins of institutions of higher education to prepare students as whole selves deserving to build their capacity for sustained quality of purpose as integral to the sense of self, for the sense of motivation to persist, and the responsibility to act for the common good.

In 2015, the Okanagan Charter is the latest charter to address health promotion on college campuses on an international level. It is a culmination of work starting with the Ottawa Charter (1985) and includes the Bangkok Charter for Health Promotion in a Globalized World (2005), the Millennium Goals (WHO 2000) and the Civil Society Initiative. It also includes previous work from the first International Conference on Health Promoting Universities in 1996, the Pan American Region in 2003, and finally the Edmonton Charter from 2005.

The Okanagan charter calls on institutions of higher education to serve two goals. Firstly universities must embed health into all aspects of campus culture, across the administration, operations, and academic mandates. Secondly universities must lead health promotion action and collaboration locally and globally. The charter states, "higher education institutions are positioned to generate, share and implement knowledge and research findings to enhance health of citizens and communities both now and in the future" (p.5, Charter). Again, the charter reiterates the responsibility of well-being on the college campus, "health promotion is not just the responsibility of the health sector but must engage all sectors to take an explicit stance in favor of health, equity, social justice and sustainability for all, while recognizing that the well-being of people, places and the planet are interdependent" (p. 4, Charter). These foundation documents provide the basis for institution governance, policy development, funding allocations, operations, and academic considerations for colleges to address health promotion across the globe.

Working across systems as complex as institutions of higher education to transform is challenging. The Okanagan Charter provides the call to action, and the collective impact framework by Christens and Tran Inzeo (2015) offers a method to implement the change. By studying a community-based obesity prevention effort and a comprehensive education reform as case studies, the value of collective impact shows it can be used in overall health promotion as well.

Collective impact distinguishes itself from coalition building and traditional collaboration models in part due to the systems-level intervention's five conditions for success. The five conditions are

1. A common agenda
2. Shared measurements
3. Mutually reinforcing activities
4. Continuous communication
5. Infrastructure support

These five conditions create the environment for change. The three steps in the collective impact are 1. Initiate action, 2. Organize for impact, 3. Sustain action and impact. The success of the collective impact approach has led to changes in grant-making models for public health initiatives. Collective impact has shown to be more disciplined and a higher performing approach for systems-level social impact. This model provides a way for universities to implement actions outlined in the Okanagan Charter for health promotion.

6

Well-being Practices on the College Campus

Holistic wellness programs are critical to the support of college students, faculty, staff, and the greater community as outlined in the Okanagan Charter. In this section, I review the literature on the recent practices and workshops that highlight recent trends and current discourse of student well-being on the college campus.

In fall 2018, I was selected to be part of the Graduate Associate Program (GAP) sponsored by NASPA which is a program designed to promote leadership opportunities for graduate students interested in the field of student affairs. Being a GAP member, I was provided access to NASPA professional development opportunities which included the chance to volunteer as a program reviewer of workshops and presentations for the upcoming 2019 NASPA Annual Conference, which coincided with the 1^{00}th anniversary of the founding of the NAPSA organization. I reviewed over 50 workshops and panel presentations related to health and wellness promotion on colleges campuses. From these 50 programs, I selected 6 programs to review in detail to analyze the role of holistic health and wellness in current programs and services offered on college campuses to understand gaps that exist in current practices. These 6 presentations are directly related to student development and student well-being on the college campus.

Student programs and services are designed for the improvement of campus services and policy. Health, healing, and cultural competency is essential to student development in college. In the program designed by Brown (2019), there is the discussion of moving students "beyond cultural competency and towards liberation using healing and liberatory practices." Cultural competency is centered on the concept of building awareness of cultural diversity issues such as white privilege, white fragility, critical race theory, and understanding microaggressions in social institutions. Learning cultural competency is especially important for students who are part of marginalized communities such as LGBTQIA+, students of color, low-income students, and students with disabilities, and students who are military veterans. This empirical example of a student program gets to the heart of student healing, but it is lacking in the importance of addressing systematic racism, diversity, equity, and inclusion policy as well there is the need to ensure students' sense of liberation is supported at the campus policy level.

Wellman (2019) researched the role of peer educator programs designed to aid students in developing programs from the students' point of view. One such program is the Health Education Awareness Resource Team (HEART). HEART student peers are part of a training model where they "participate in an intensive training process, including a three-credit public health course that prepares them to promote student well-being, cultivate community, elevate their voices and be agents of change on campus". The program is a presentation of the challenges due to a dearth in outcomes-based approaches in peer education. Without the accountability and outcomes-based approach, the program fails to meet the professional standards of the Okanagan Charter.

There are specialized support programs within select population-based programs. The support program presented by Lozano (2019) is an example of this type of program. Many colleges offer a first-year student experience (FYE) program for freshman in undergraduate programs. This presentation focused on the emotional concerns of students in a FYE program. Three areas that were brought under one umbrella included using a wellness model, FYE, and suicide prevention. The tools that are discussed include a diagnostic, the Vulnerability Test, QPR Suicide Prevention, Habitudes, and Active Bystander training for students. These are valuable evidence-based tools for prevention and treatment of several issues of well-being for college students. What is lacking from these interventions is the connection of student-focused services as they relate to FYE academic-focused services. Where is the collaboration and integration of these programs with academic experiences of students in the FYE?

Another important area for handling student stress is self-care. Self-care is part of overall student well-being. Like the work by Brown (2019) about healing, there is a presentation by Obear (2019) about the importance of self-care and healing for campus change agents. Interestingly, this workshop is a focus on students interested in making change to create "greater equity, inclusion, and social justice on campus" yet students often find themselves "too weary or overwhelmed to make meaningful change." Students doing the work of fighting for social change on the college campus often face burnout and stress. Again, this could affect students from marginalized communities in unique ways. Many students get involved in campus activities for the sake of developing leadership skills and to improve the campus community. Yet, these students often have little in terms of support for their own self-care. This presentation focused on exploring "roots of their stress and burnout and to deepen their capacity to rejuvenate, re-energize, and retool themselves as powerful campus change agents for social justice". It is interesting to note that the presentation does not address how students from marginalized populations might feel who might be especially susceptible to stress or burn out based on having a marginalized social identity.

Health and well-being programs often refer to the social-ecology model because it goes to the heart of the environmental and human interaction's role in their influence on human behavior. Caldwell and Knight Wilt (2019) tackle the topic of healthy eating using the social-ecology model to "review how one campus has successfully incorporated services, programs, communications, environmental and policy strategies to promote and reinforce consuming a balanced diet and improve the community's attitude towards food". This all-encompassing systematic approach to healthy eating is a great example of the social-ecology model in action. In addition, the program uses evidence-based practices such as the Healthy Minds Study and the guidelines from the USDA. While the program is comprehensive and covers the spectrum of the social-ecology model from the individual to the community to policy development, there is no inclusion of cultural and diversity issues as it relates to the connection between food and behavior. Cultural and diversity issues impact students from marginalized communities including students from low-income communities in ways that must be addressed in the program.

With the data from the national health assessment on college student health and well-being demonstrating the importance of health promotion to combat the astronomically high levels of stress that college students face on college campuses, these topics that are the current trends of discussion in higher education student development indicate many gaps in services and programs. While the topics presented here are a small sample of the current research in health promotion, they are an example of the current practices in health and well-being on college campuses, nonetheless. Finally, it is important to note that not one college or university in the United Sates has adopted the Okanagan Charter as an institution even after over 18 colleges in Canada have adopted it.

The next section will be a discussion of the solution I see as part of the answer to the gaps in services on college campuses.

7

The Nurturing Framework on the College Campus

While attending an institution of higher education is one step on a lifelong journey of learning and developing skills to live a full life, the environment of higher education continues to struggle in finding new and different ways to support students, especially for non-traditional and disadvantaged students, and to enhance all students' sense of overall health and well-being. The period of college is when many young adults independently face serious health issues for the very first time around risky health choices such as nutrition, sex, drugs, sleep, exercise, smoking, mental health, and other health behaviors that can lead to lifelong habits or vices that should be acknowledged in the setting of higher education. More recently, colleges and universities have provided support to address the risky health behavior of college students, but a gap in the services and support remains for holistic-based practices and for support of the overall well-being of students, especially for non-traditional and disadvantaged students. Just as importantly, by intentionally aiding college students in their health and well-being development, institutions of higher education can truly become environments where students learn how to optimize their academic performance and overall development of self.

Colleges can work toward these goals by providing instruction, policy, and peer support programs that support undergraduate holistic health and well-being. In the following sections of this book, I introduce an 11-week course syllabus designed to focus on a model that I created called the Nurturing Framework model for use in higher education for student health and well-being. I will also discuss how the NF model can apply to the set of nationally recognized standards by the Council for the Advancement of Standards in Higher Education (CAS) on student well-being programs, and how schools can operationalize the NF for a peer-to-peer program to support student development.

8

Creating the Nurturing Framework Model

Throughout my coursework in the Holistic Health Education program at John F. Kennedy University, the process of healthy change and the process of maintaining health behavior change has been central to discussions and practices in program courses to develop better understanding of holistic health education. I developed the Nurturing Framework model out of my coursework, health education internship experience, and program requirements. The model is also based off research gathered from a student survey developed through one of my graduate classes. The survey consisted of 10 questions about the mind/body/spirit/community and was completed by fellow students in the Master of Arts program in the Holistic Health Education program. The model is a holistic-based approach to supporting healthy behaviors of college students by addressing the four domains in the Nurturing Framework (NF) model. The NF model represents an approach to supporting health and wellness practices of undergraduates using the intention of the holistic perspective. The model is a healthy change model based on the four domains of Nurturing, like the four walls of a room. There should always be intentional space for well-being on the college campus. The domains consist of the four **SIDES** of the Room for Well-being, **S**ensing Domain, **I**nternal Domain, **D**oing Domain, and **E**xternal Domain.

Figure 2: Nurturing Framework Model

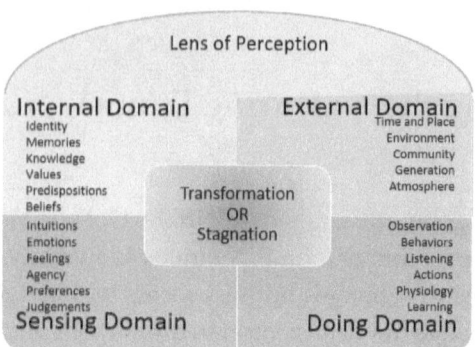

For students to transform using this Nurturing Framework model, students must develop their sense of perception to have conscious understanding of the influence of their actions and choices on their sense of well-being and as a self-directed student. The lens of perception is the overarching key to the ability of a student to recognize and act in the four domains which are necessary for change to take place. If there are domains that do not apply to a transition point, then the student will remain in a state of stagnation. In this model, progress and resistance are both included within the definition of transformation. The transformation can be either negative or positive. For example, if during a period of growth, a student has all four domains present and refuses to change or is resistance to healthy change, then the student experiences a negative transformation at that point. An example of this experience might be a student who is abusing alcohol or drugs and is seeking treatment at a rehabilitation center. The student has the choice to receive treatment and make positive changes to continue with their college experience, or they can decide to continue to live as an addict. The model, which can be used to develop assessment tools, provides a method of understanding how a negative transformation is a result of all four domains being present for positive change, yet the student's resistance means the student has failed in the transformation process to quit the negative health behavior. The same can happen with college students who have access to support programs and services yet drop out of college. A student self-questionnaire can be developed using the model to help students self-reflect. As well, the model can be used to develop a climate survey for a higher education institution for self-study. There could be support programs for undergraduates to bolster up their four areas of nurturing domains or students could work to develop their lens of perception to develop awareness of nurturing support programs that support positive transformation.

9

Student Facing and Institution Facing Support Using the Nurturing Framework

Many colleges have student development programs and services that address topics of special interest to college students such as racial and gender identity development, time management, career/life planning, choosing a major, and other activities that support the student's development of their sense of self as a college student. In the area of student services, programs, services, and activities are important as extracurricular and co-curricular options. Yet in terms of providing concentrated focus on a single course subject, a college course differentiates itself from co-curriculars by the level of quality of attention and support provided by an academic professional trained in the subject matter. In providing a college class on the topic of nurturing, health and well-being practices for college students based on the Nurturing Framework, students will develop tools and resources to truly get the most out of their higher education experience.

I envision a Nurturing Framework course, an 11-week course, offered to entering students - either freshman or first-year students or newly transferred students from other colleges and universities. It can also be a course that is adapted for specialized populations such as military veterans, single parents, immigrants/refugees, and first-generation students, students of color, LGBTQIA+, students with disabilities, re-entry students, low income students, and senior-year students. Any undergraduate who is beginning or ending a degree program with the college would be encouraged to enroll in the course. By offering this material across an 11-week course, it would be suitable as a class for any academic calendar either semester or quarter length. As well, it could be scheduled as a late-start or summer bridge course to help students make the transition to college.

The key components of the course are the one-on-one advising and the holistic units around mind, body, spirit, and community. The course can be taught by a holistic health education professional with a Master of Art degree in holistic health education and knowledge, experience, and familiarity with college student development theories. The course should be limited in size to no more than 25 students per class. The limitation in size is to encourage the development of a strong relationship between the students and the instructor and to facilitate the development of community in the course. As well, the initial part of the program is one-on-one advising completed by the instructor to provide a baseline for the students in their over health and wellness behaviors. The course has the following course schedule of topics:

Week 1 – one-on-one health and wellness advising
Weeks 2-4 – Mind Unit
Weeks 5-7 – Body Unit
Weeks 8-10 – Spirit Unit
Week 11 – Community Unit and community goal setting

In the following sections there will be more detail about the components for the course units.

10

A Course Outline Using the Nurturing Framework

Individual advising is a key component of the class because it is about finding a personalized approach to motivation. Many students in college are creating and developing their habits, behaviors, and sense of self for the first time on their own. In the college setting many students face questions about their identity and why they are the way they are. There is the potential for tremendous growth during the college years because all assumptions are questioned and challenged when compared with other students in the setting of higher education. Based on the NF, personalized support is critical during this period. The individual advising is about finding the strengths of the students and developing goals, aspirations, and targets to achieve as a new college student. The individualized planning session at the beginning and again at the end of the class is a way to support and hold the student accountable to their personalized and community-based goals.

Mind Unit

To develop and maintain healthy mental habits is the goal with this unit of the class. Using various components of salutogenesis theory, this unit will focus on the core areas of sense of coherence (Antonovsky, 1987), flow (Csikszentmihalyi, 2104), well-being (Diener, 1984), empowerment (Freire, 2004), learned optimism (Seligman, 2006) and ecological system theory (Bronfenmrenner, 1979). Students will have exposure to theories that underscore the importance of finding purpose, satisfaction, and personal meaning. These theories help to address some of the major issues facing students under stress, namely thoughts of suicide or self-harm, feelings of anxiety, loneliness, and loss of connection and loss of focus. This unit aligns with the Internal Domain in the NF model.

Embodiment Unit

To develop and maintain healthy physical/physiologically related habits is the goal with this unit. Using other salutogenesis theories the students will understand the importance of the mind body connection in overall health. Theories about action competence (Jensen, 1994) address health and wellness of the body. The notion of competence is linked to the Self-Determination Theory (Deci and Ryan, 2004) and shows that three elements of competence provide intrinsic and external motivation to boost positive outcomes. The three elements are autonomy, relatedness, and competency. These theories help address some of the major issues facing students including drug or alcohol abuse, headaches, neck, and back pain, eating disorders, indigestion, addictions, over exercising and weight gain. This unit aligns with the Doing Domain in the NF model.

Spiritual Unit

To develop and maintain healthy spiritual habits is the goal with this unit. These salutogenesis theories help students understand the importance of the spiritual arena in their role as students in higher education. Theories about gratitude (Emmons and McCullough, 2004), empathy (Eisenberg, 1990), attachment (Bolby, 2008), learned hopefulness (Zimmerman, 1990), and spiritual connection provide alignment and coherence for students and their personal and academic achievement. These theories help address some of the major issues facing college students including procrastinating, hopelessness, and loss of motivation. This unit aligns with the Sensing Domain in the NF model.

Chapter 10

Community Unit

To develop and practice community centered habits is the goal of this unit. The basis for salutogenesis is the notion of social connection because it is at the core of all healthy habits for long lasting healthy behavior and long life. The theories that would be covered include social and emotional intelligence (Goleman, 2006) and quality of life (Eriksson and Lindstrom, 2007) highlighting the importance of taking an active role in building community for all to thrive. The inclusion of connectedness (Blum, 2005) supports the sense of relatedness to the individual and student community's purpose in college. These theories work to address issues facing undergraduates such as drinking, smoking, drug abuse, academic discipline, physical and verbal violence, and isolation. This unit aligns with the External Domain in the NF model.

11

Policy Based on the Nurturing Framework

For students to truly experience support for their overall health and well-being, there must be a policy directive for these types of programs and services across higher education institutions from inside the classroom to the community outside the classroom. There must be college-wide policy to support health and wellness.

CAS Standards are used in the development of college level policy and have an impact on administration of programs and services such as staffing levels, budgeting levels, facilities, and space designation, hiring practices, job descriptions, and in the "development, assessment, and improvement of quality student learning, programs, and services" (NASPA, 2018). These standards impact professional standards and quality assurance for staff and faculty working with students. The lack of the inclusion of holistic foundations in health and well-being standards means that organizations are not truly meeting the needs of the whole student. CAS standards must include a holistic and salutogenesis framework to address health and well-being behaviors for students to optimize their personal and academic achievement.

Institutions of higher education benefit from having a healthy student population. Many institutions have implemented CAS policy for various programs and services. Several CAS standards are currently available for various health-related topics including Alcohol and Other Drug Programs, Sexual Violence-Related Programs and Services, Health Promotion Services, Clinical Health Services, and Academic Advising Programs (CAS, 2019). In 2017, there was the development of a CAS standard titled

Preventing High-Risk Behaviors and Building Healthy Campuses. While this is a sorely needed step in the right direction, the CAS standard does not include a wellness-based solution to high-risk behavior. As well, according to recent mental health assessment data (ACHA, 2019) there are far more students suffering from anxiety, depression, and other mental health issues than the risky behaviors that are often the focus of the CAS standards.

In the following section, I'll discuss how holistic practices can provide a solution based on salutogenesis and social-ecology model for supporting healthy behavior and well-being practices across institutions of higher education.

12

Campus Community Development Based on the Nurturing Framework Model

The importance of social support on overall health and wellness is well-known. In the college setting, peer support programs are the community of support many students need to maintain and keep up with goals and motivation. The beauty of providing a peer support program for health-related programs is the savings on costs for staffing and the flexibility of scheduling due to abundant staffing availability. Peer support programs can be staffed with second- and third-year students or even graduate students to provide additional support for students in their personal journey. By having peer support, students expand their social connections across the campus. In addition to supporting healthy behaviors, peer support provides an opportunity for students to develop skills in the health education field. Students using services and acting as peer support staff gain the opportunity to learn about the health education field and career opportunities available through the practices of health and wellness. As well, the peer support staff can develop relationships with other college staff and can have access to information about joining professional associations having to do with health and wellness. As well, as part of the CAS standards of health promotion programs, the staff would have the benefit of conducting evaluations and assessments of the program to gain experience in research and program development.

A peer support program can take many forms. The program could provide any of the following services on student health and wellness: workshops, group sessions, individual advising, printed materials, website content, social media, a resource library, community outings, trainings, professional development, research, reports, classroom presentations, recognition ceremony, calendar of events, print media, press releases, and other activities to promote the importance of health and wellness for optimizing student personal and academic achievement. These services being available for students on a drop-in basis or by appointment could provide the personalized support students' needs as they navigate their development of self.

A peer support program could function as an arm of the college health services already in place at most college campuses. Often health services staff and professionals are too overwhelmed with health crises, scares, and daily services to provide specialized programming. Health and wellness programming is often considered a luxury to the necessary services provided on a college campus. Yet research shows that a focus on the health and wellness of student experience leads to deeper sense of satisfaction, purpose, meaning, and stress reduction, thereby serving as a preventative measure to the costs of risky health behaviors (Antonovsky, 1987, Seligman, 2006).

# 13

Summary

The rising rates of anxiety and depression on the college campus mean that services and programs to address this epidemic can no longer be considered the sole responsibility of the college health center. Just as health promotion in general is no longer considered the sole responsibility of medical centers across the country, the importance of health promotion and student well-being transcends the traditional divisions across college campus departments. The solution provided in this book takes this perspective in addressing overall stress management with a class curriculum based on the Nurturing Framework model for practices, as well as student well-being coaching, and updating college service policy standards to include the Nurturing Framework.

The solutions are based on the model I designed called the Nurturing Framework Model which include the four domains that make up the four walls in the Room for Student Well-being, Sensing, Internal, Doing, and External (SIDEs). The salutogenesis and social ecology models continue in the same vein of student development theories that focus on student identity development and learning environment development. These theories and the NF model support health promotion and student well-being on the college campus.

Salutogenesis is like the yellow brick road through the Land of Oz. It is an umbrella term that encompasses many different topics or assets for health and well-being. At the core of the theory is the belief that one can shape their health by building up or strengthening assets of health. The solution proposed would build the student's sense of their health through an 11-week course, and peer coaching. The college programs and services would build their capacity to support health through changes in CAS standards to include the Nurturing Framework model.

With the advancement of mobile technology and personalized learning, there is a strong opportunity for a holistic approach for stress reduction on the college campus. Already there are apps on phones to help students with stress reduction. Many college campuses are devoting resources, staff, and funding for real health promotion practices. What is missing is an integral approach that works across instructional and student services operations. With more competencies being defined through policy standards for health promotion and focus on student well-being, there really is no limit to the programs and services that can be developed.

The next step for these new programs and services is systematic assessment and measurements of success. There is the National College Health Assessment (NCHA) that is a useful measure of health, but there needs to be a complimentary assessment of Nurturing interventions on the college campus. Perhaps with the higher visibility and awareness of the epidemic of college student health, there will be better attention paid to successful intervention strategies for comparisons and measures. With healthy practices taking a more active role on college campuses hopefully more students can thrive on the other side of the rainbow.

Part II

Nurturing Our Self in Everyday Life

14

Sleep

Sleep is a wonder drug. As much as sleep is enjoyable, it fulfills essential bodily and mental functions. Sleep is necessary for all living things. It is not simply about rest, enjoyment, and quiet solitude. Sleep has amazing powers!

Sleep is basically when the mind/body does a complete mental, emotional, and physical overhaul. During a good quality sleep is when the body is rejuvenated and recharged. The role of sleep has been linked to brain functions such as memory and learning as well as many functions of the body from repair to regeneration of tissues, to strengthening the immune system and building bones and muscles. Poor sleeping patterns is linked to an increase in mortality and other health problems such as high blood pressure, obesity, heart attack, stroke, and mood disorders (Porter, 2019).

Thousands of years ago ancient civilizations recognized the power of sleep. Ancient traditional medical practices underscore the importance of the mind body connection and the role of sleep in our daily lives.

Ayurveda is a mind body medicine that is receiving renewed interest in its application to treat sleep disorders. The Chopra Center is a research institute that develops practices based on Ayurveda principles that can aid in sleep disorders.

Exciting developments in mind body medicine research shows the power of the body to support its own healing. In the last 20 years there has been a plethora of research that shows how effective mind body medicine is in the treatment of sleep disorders.

Effective Mind Body Medicine Treatments for Sleep Disorders

Developing healthy sleep hygiene and learning about relaxation methods have been an extremely effective evidence-based mind body medicine practice for sleep disorders. Vincent and Lewycky (2009) studied over 100 adults with chronic insomnia. They offered an invention that consisted of online education about sleep hygiene and stimulus control. The results were that the treatment "produced improvements in the primary end points of sleep quality" and the severity of insomnia and daytime fatigue were noticeably reduced, as well as "dysfunctional beliefs about sleep" (Vincent and Lewycky, 2009).

In the research by Irwin et al. (2008), over 100 older adults with moderate sleep complaints learned about the importance of sleep and health education, along with T'ai Chi Chih practice. Subjects showed improvements using the Pittsburgh Sleep Quality Index. The sleep patterns of the participants improved in duration, efficiency, and less sleep disturbances.

In a comparison between use of a placebo and health education on sleep, the study by Soeffing et al. (2008) experimented with over 40 older adults with chronic insomnia. The intervention consisted of sleep health education, 7.5-mg of zopiclone nightly or placebo medication. Over six months the three groups sleep patterns were tracked. The group that learned about sleep hygiene had better sleep patterns and efficiency than those taking the placebo and the zopliclone, though the total sleep time was similar across all three groups.

Other researchers found that sleep health education was enough for greater sleep efficiencies and in reducing sleep disturbances for people suffering from sleep disorders (Carney et al., 2003; Goodwin et al, 2004; Irwin et al., 2008; Jarrin et al., 2013; Lichstein et al, 2001; Waters et al., 2011).

In addition to health education about sleep hygiene, other mind body practices have shown success in treating sleep disorders.

Harmat et al. (2008) in a study with 94 college students with sleep complaints looked at the use of classical music or audiobook, versus no intervention for improving sleep. Using a sleep quality scale, students who listened to classical music showed significantly improved sleep quality over the other two groups.

In a study by Manjunath and Telles (2005) 120 older adults tried yoga, herbal medicine, versus a control group who did not change their sleep habits. The group who used yoga saw significant improvement in sleep habits including decrease in length of time to fall asleep, increase in total numbers of hours asleep, and overall feeling of being rested after rising in the morning even up to 6 months after treatment.

In another study by Lichstein et al. (2001), 89 older adults with insomnia were treated with the intervention of relaxation practices, sleep compression, or placebo desensitization. Sleep compression was found to be most effective, but all intervention showed improved self-reported sleep, though objective sleep was unchanged.

Not all mind body interventions have shown success. Pallesen et al., (2003) conducted a study with 55 older adults with insomnia. The group was provided with education about sleep hygiene, stimulus reduction, and the control group was provided with relaxation recordings. There was no difference between the two groups after the interventions.

Sleep Health Education and Practices

The evidence-based practices that support mind body medicine is overwhelmingly positive. As a graduate student intern, I was able to use these practices in my work. I have been working in the field of college student services for over 15 years. I have mostly concentrated my career in the delivery of technical support to students in the college admissions process. Recently, I was able to develop practices to support student well-being through my graduate student internship.

Learning About Sleep for Students

To support student sleep hygiene, I developed a self-care curriculum. I provided an opportunity for students to reflect on their own sleep practices. There is also a mindfulness component to show ways to pay attention and be attuned to the connection between their decisions about time management and how those decisions impact sleep habits. As well, I encouraged students to develop a sleep plan.

With sleep, there is the need to reduce distractions and to understand the importance of a regular sleep schedule. Like many adults, students have false beliefs and misinformation about the amount of sleep that is necessary for proper brain and memory function. It is important to provide resources and documentation, so students understand that recent research supports the importance of sleep hygiene. One class at a time, I had the opportunity to help students change the way they think about sleep.

Sleep truly is a wonder drug. It is free, fun, and fulfills a basic health requirement for the betterment of all our lives. Everyone can do their part in shaping our environment and beliefs for better sleep habits. Better sleep means better health!

15

Personal Dignity

The personal dignity around updated pronouns and names cannot be emphasized enough. LGBTQIA+ health disparities among our youth can be addressed in part through a collaborative effort among the state's public education systems to implement the National Culturally and Linguistically Appropriate Services (NCLAS) Standards across K-16 sectors. There is ample evidence to demonstrate that LGBTQIA+ health disparities are linked to higher rates of homelessness, poverty, bias, stigma, discrimination, and lack of insurance coverage because of lack of cultural competence within state public education systems (Out2Enroll).

As well, mental health disparities among LGBTQIA+ youth show suicide rates more than three times the national average, twice the reported rates of being bullied, and higher rates of substance abuse and twice the rates of mental health disorders as compared to national rates. Psychological factors of feeling unsafe includes facing discrimination, harassment, and lack of cultural competency results in LGBTQIA+ students having higher rates of absenteeism from school. It is imperative that LGBTQIA+ youth benefit from the NCLAS Standards in the development of programs and services in our public education system.

NCLAS Standards established in 2000 and enhanced in 2013 were developed to provide services that are respectful and responsive to each person's culture and communication needs, as well as guidelines for governance and policy. It has been shown that public schools understand and value the importance of providing culturally and linguistically responsive policy as it relates to English language learners in assessment and classroom instruction. The National Association for the Education of Young Children (NAEYC) developed guidelines for the assessment of young English language learners which provides a framework for how NCLAS standards could benefit the classroom for instruction that can similarly be used to address awareness of LGBTQIA+ considerations in services.

Among the recommendations provided by NAEYC as it relates to culturally and linguistically appropriate services is the support for expanding the knowledge base of our student demographics, developing comprehensive assessments, increasing the numbers of culturally competent faculty and staff and professional development in effective assessment for special populations of students. These are recommendations that could be used as a framework for our work with LGBTQIA+ youth in our public schools as well.

Fortunately, New Hampshire Department of Education (NHDE) provides a working model of successful implementation of the use of NCLAS in the wellness program across the state that is in alignment with the Safe Schools/Healthy Students federal program along with other health projects (i.e. Project AWARE, NH System of Care, Every Moment Counts Occupational Therapy, Project GROW: Integrating Resilience, Outcomes, & Wellness, and Collaborative Innovative Network), which provide support and professional development for teachers and staff.

The program includes a full-time staff member with the title Cultural, Linguistic Competency Coordinator who works across the district's schools to provide training and support to local programs and services. Inclusive in the program design and recommendations is a Self-Assessment Checklist for Personnel Providing Programs and Support for LGBTQIA+ Youth and their Families. The services and support are available for the classroom, school, and district. It addresses the individual, class, school, and community using the principals of the social ecology model to develop influential programs and practices to address health. Statewide models should serve as an example to address LGBTQIA+ issues across all Departments of Education.

Public education can lead the way in addressing health disparities in the LGBTQIA+ youth through use of the CLAS Standards in our public education system. This policy would support the current initiative to support social and emotional learning as well as the initiative to provide safe haven schools which includes safety for sexual orientation and sexual identity issues facing students. The 2014 School Health Policies and Practices Study (SHPPS) found that only 17% of high school health service coordinators received professional development about LGB student health and that only 38% of high schools had Gay-Straight Alliances. In addition to failing to include transgender student health data in the services and programs at the high school, there is *no data* about culturally and linguistically appropriate services provided in the primary or secondary programs. Addressing the disparities for LGBTQIA+ students would mean authentically safe schools and healthy students from all our students including LGBTQIA+ students.

How can CLAS Standards work across the nation's public education system?

CLAS considers health beliefs, preferred languages, healthy literacy levels, and communication needs for culturally and linguistically appropriate services that includes LGBTQIA+ issues. With the inclusion of CLAS in public education, performance indicators would see an increase in respect, understanding, effectiveness, and equity in programs and services. CLAS can aid in moving the public education system in a step in the right direction to provide services and programs for all students to have a safe, healthy, and authentic learning environment for the sake of our students' personal dignity.

16

Stress Reduction and the Type A personality

The Type A personality first recognized by Friedman and Rosenman (1957) faces unique challenges when dealing with stress. The Type A personality on the job and in the school years must take care to learn how to adjust to a new and challenging environment. In education, there are "Super Students" that have been on high alert all through their formal education. Learning some tips about stress relief for this specific personality can go a long way to avoiding burnout, anxiety, depression, and other common ailments of employees and students.

What is the Type A Personality?

Knowing your own personality or the personality of your friends, roommate, classmates, and others can help you navigate the relationships you have with others. Personality traits of people with a Type A Personality include impatience, impulsiveness, easily angered/annoyed, short temper, competitiveness, overly time conscious, demanding, tense, perfectionist, ambitious, tightly wound, and negatively self-critical.

Characteristics of the Type A Personality

Many of the behaviors that are rewarded with high grades that can lead to college attendance cause challenges later as a college student. Behaviors such as talking fast, micromanaging time schedule, being a workaholic, interrupting others, physical fidgets/tics, leg bounce, finger tapping, domineering, intolerant of being a team player, often end up resulting in high stress college life, careers and experiencing high job dissatisfaction as an adult.

What Are the Health Risks of a Type A Personality?

In college and later in life, knowing your personality can help you avoid negative outcomes for the Type A Personality. Known health factors for this personality include higher risk for stroke, heart disease, consumption of high amounts of caffeine, development of bad habits for health like smoking, compromised quality of sleep, irregular heartbeat, and poor anger management.

Why Don't People with Type A Personality Just Relax?

Unfortunately, because of the high level of productivity, many people view many attributes of the Type A personality as aspirational in the fast-paced world of work in the United States. Personality traits like natural competitiveness often led to generally higher levels of physical fitness, working long hours, and the need to constantly prove oneself. Yet it is the unhealthy habits that are the problem, not only the high-risk health factors. Having an intense personality is not the issue, but anger management that can lead to risky behavior. Consequently, convincing a Type A personality person to change habits to avoid heart disease and mental health issues is often not sufficient rationale for changing behavior. One of the ironies is that Type A personalities can view self-care and relaxation as a waste of time.

What Happens When the Type A Personality Goes Overboard?

After the Type A runs on all cylinders for too long, you can expect a crash. Exhaustion and sleep deprivation affects energy and motivation. Cortisol in blood negatively affects memory over time. Lowered concentration leads to mistakes, errors, bad judgement. Reduction in creativity, problem solving, and innovative thinking. Negative relationships diminish social and work relationships. Constant muscle tensions lead to low back pain, sciatica, neck, and shoulder aches. Negative health behaviors, such as pulling an all-night work session, trigger stress hormones disrupt digestion, and leads to ulcers, colitis, and irritable bowel syndrome. Appetite swings from overwork trigger metabolic changes and weight gain. Stress from overwork lowers the immune system, leads to skin breakouts, and hair loss. Another reaction to overload of work can be impotence and reduced enjoyment in sex.

So, how do you convince someone who is highly productive, competitive, driven to succeed and rewarded with good grades and social/academic rewards to find time for stress relief? The trick is to match the stress relief with the personality. Stress relief does not have to be boring or time consuming!

Stress relief with coursework
Limit number of tasks in a day to no more than 5 tasks
Break assignments into manageable goals
Complete important tasks first
Take frequent breaks
Give credit to self for completing tasks and re-prioritize for the next day
Exchange tasks that are longer term rather than adding more to the list

Stress relief in everyday life
Exercise that is fast-paced or intense such as spinning, hot yoga, rock climbing, running, cross-fit, hip-hop dancing etc.
Music that is fast-paced and upbeat, include singing aloud if possible
Invite friends over
Find a new high energy hobby or continue a forgotten one like skateboarding, skydiving, mountain biking, graffiti, etc.

Write/journal creative expressions or songwriting
Breathing exercises including laughter sessions

Stress relief with the community
Charity or giving to others
Compete in a poetry slam or standup comedy or improv
Daily walking in a group
Socialize with others/join social clubs
Explore new places/travel with a group i.e. Events and adventures
Spend time in nature/appreciating the outdoors through a community class
Attend/volunteer for social/community events

Today in the Covid pandemic, everyone experiences stress at higher rates than ever before. The good news is that more and more school and work settings are taking into consideration college student well-being more than ever before. Lastly, learning about the different personality types, everyone can learn tricks to stress relief that don't take away from their fast-paced lifestyle.

17

Physical Activity

I have always prided myself on being athletic and strong when it comes to taking on a physically demanding challenge. Over the years I have been able to complete 10 K races and go on long hikes into the woods and feel fine I am getting older (45 this year!), so the things I used to do with my body are not the same as in years past. In the last year, with job uncertainties and an unpredictable schedule I have not been able to keep up with any type of regular physical activity. Even so, I have felt that my energy is strong. So, I try as much as I can to do physical exercise throughout the day, even if it only involves taking the stairs instead of the elevator.

One thing that has been on my side is that my parents and family has always prided themselves on daily physical activity.

My dad used to take us as children on long arduous walks along the horse trails behind our house. Being little children, we were sometimes dragged along for what felt like hours and often ended the long walk-in tears because of the time and effort it took to complete these outings. It was no simple stroll, but a death hike, because we never knew how long it would last. Still, these physical feats prepared me to push myself and my mental stamina.

These kinds of memories came in handy two months ago when my car decided to break down. I was without a car or a means to get to work so I needed to ride my bike to work.

At first, I wasn't sure if I had it in me to make the 6-mile bike ride each way to and from work. After all, I hadn't ridden a bike in years. Not even a stationary bike.

Still, I approached the physical challenge with a sense of curiosity and wonder.

Could I still do this even at my age and physical condition?

This is something I used to do as a teenager, take a bike and ride for an hour, no preparation. Just go!

The stress of getting to work on time made me a nervous wreck, but my body was up to the challenge. My mind was made up that I could do this, like any other challenge. It was all about having a positive attitude and having mental stamina! As a child I went on those death hikes without any option or position to argue. Now, I was in command, in the driver's seat. My body was ready to take on this challenge. I rode my bike to work 6 miles in each direction for three days. It was an unexpected challenge, but I knew I could not let myself down.

How did it go?

It was hard but I proved to myself I still got it! Plus, I made myself proud for sticking to it! Challenge yourself each day. You never know when you might need to push yourself to the limit.

18

My Father's Experience of Gratitude

An American Motorcyclist in Japan.
Re-printed from Japan Quarterly, 1961.
By Donald Ploski *(my father)*

Having spent my entire service tour at a radar site in Ōminato, a small fishing village kitty-cornered across Mutsu Bay from Aomori, I felt, as the time for discharge neared, a strong desire to see other parts of Japan. Restricted to northern Honshū, I had been as isolated as if I had remained in America. Thus, I decided to travel by motorcycle and see at first-hand the nine-hundred kilometer stretch of Japan between the Tsugaru straits and my new home in Atami.

Both my Japanese and American friends warned me that such a trip was not without its dangers. The American fears ranged from doubt that the route could be found without a great waste of time, to a dimpled, double-chinned WAC Captain who clutched my wrist and said, "But they tell me there are bandits on the road at night!" Wild tales would she tell once she got back to Columbus, Ohio.

My Japanese friends were much more practical, advising me to carry all the spare parts I could, as well as a notebook containing in English, Rōmaji and Japanese messages for all possible emergencies. Surprisingly, as I traveled further away from Ōminato, even some of the more common requests, that my northern friends had no difficulty understanding, puzzled some of my would-be informants on the road south. Many times, English was more easily understood than the Tsugaru-tainted

Japanese I had dutifully memorized in northern Honshū.

I went well prepared. Allowing for every possible emergency (with the exception of meeting bandits) I fully loaded a packboard with such things as: A Swedish stove, mosquito net, survival kit, tow cable, canned food, rain covers, knives, flashlights and, topping it all, a down-filled sleeping bag guaranteed to sixty degrees below zero. Since I was making the trip in the middle of August, this last item struck even me as being just a bit over-suspicious of the peculiarities of the Japanese terrain. When I strapped this outfit on my back, it almost buckled my knees. Nevertheless, I was content that whatever the temperamental Japanese gods had in store for me, fire, earthquake, or typhoon, I would be prepared.

I left at dawn. Ōminato, like most of the other drab Aomori Prefecture towns that squat on the side of the sea, has only one productive interest besides the rolling ocean: its rice fields. As I balanced the weight of my pack, the dawn sun touched with orange the green rice sprouts and the quiet waves of Mutsu Bay. The dirt road was deserted save for an occasional farmer and his cart. White whisps of morning mist hung low in the fallow valleys. The noise of my motorcycle accentuated the particular silence that Japanese villages seem to have at daybreak. After some minutes the road took a sharp bend to the south. I had traveled as far east as I would go on the entire trip. The morning sunlight was on my left shoulder and Tokyo was eight hundred and fifty kilometers in front of me. I stopped and looked to my right. Miles across Mutsu Bay I saw the gradual slope of Mount Kamabuse. In my mind's eye only, I could distinguish, perched on the summit, the two white globes that marked the radar site where I had spent two snow-filled winters in my early twenties. A brocade of indistinct gray blocks at the base of the mountain was Ōminato, all I knew of Japan so far. At that moment, I felt like a Hokaidō country boy going to Tokyo for the first time to seek his fortune. With a last salute to my Kamabuse Yama,

Ōminato and all things military, I started south again with a roar.

Although my map assured me, I was on a grade one main road, knee-deep ruts, unmarked turns, and branches cluttered the way. Additional hazards were flocks of scavenging chickens, wandering cattle and decrepit, lurching school buses. The greatest danger, however, were horse-drawn carts driven by bearded farmers who unfailingly executed a movement that is known in basketball circles as a hip fake, every time I tried to pass them. They would start for the right side of the road until I committed myself, then they would violently cut to the left. This maneuver usually found me with front and back brake grinding helplessly, the breaking action on soft mud nil, with a choice of three escape routes:

Striking the back brake just prior to entering the impact area, one could conceivably go into an angled, side-skid between the legs and under the abdomen of the horse. This I never tried, though I would be the first to admit its theoretical possibility.

Inches in front of the chest and under the nose of the horse.

Take the water route and go into the small stream that parallels most Japanese roads.

The second choice calls for the utmost in mass-velocity calculations as well as a violent wrenching of the head to the left as you approach the collision point. When done with verve, it is daring and picturesque. However, after a brown mare, south of Noheji, reared in panic at the delicate moment, leaving grooves in the top of my helmet, I decided to specialize in the third method of escape.

The success of this rested on many things: the first the geological composition of the bottom, as well as the depth of the water, and of course, my own speed and balance. This maneuver, when well executed, was flamboyant and soul-satisfying. There would be the tense moment when wagon, horse and driver were caught turned to the left completely blocking the road to the motorcycle. Tragedy? No, for unhesitatingly the steel-nerved cyclist would plunge into the ditch. A sheet of white water would burst in front of the vehicle as, with a low-throated roar, it leapt back onto the road and continued on its way. However, if the depth was too great, ah then! There were angry words and obscene gestures exchanged, vendettas sworn, and pedestrians forced to help pull both sputtering rider and motorcycle from the depths. My final solution was not one that pleased me, but it was safer, if less spectacular. I would approach every cart like a fighter pilot identifying a civilian airliner. Within one hundred yards I beeped my horn every ten seconds. This warning enabled my man and his draft animal to go through their full repertoire of parade maneuvers well before our distance interval became critical. Then, positive he was where he wanted to be, I would dash past. This system worked best of all.

As I continued south the road became more cosmopolitan. Now an occasional private car was seen in contrast to the purely utilitarian milk trucks, carts and school buses that had been my only companions thus far. After five hours of kidney-bruising ridges, I found myself on the first pavement I had driven on, outside of town roads, in a year and a half. Who could guess you could ride so smoothly and silently? In a burst of gratitude, for it was a fine sun that day, I vowed to compose a sonnet "To the Seventeen Miles of Concrete Pavement Outside Morioka, Japan."

The landscape too changed perceptibly. Instead of flat rice fields stretching to gray mountains, short hills and tightly terraced gardens crowded in on the road. Tall eucalyptus and pines shaded lush grass fields, so different from the scraggly northern briers. Toward evening I stopped at a restaurant with a bamboo grove behind it. There is no green more living, more sensual than the green of a bamboo grove with a slight wind moving through it. Face stinging from wind burn, and still blinking away grains of sand that had struck my goggles miles behind, I

Chapter 18

relaxed, and the coolness seduced my spirit. I thought - now I am really in Japan. I have found the scented East Joseph Conrad wrote about. For a moment I stood expectantly in the twilight, perhaps unconsciously awaiting the arrival of the humming-bird beauty of some love-saddened geisha.

I found the city of Sendai at eight-thirty that evening. "Found" is accurate. I distinctly remember passing one policeman three times before finding a road out of his neighborhood. After a light supper, I wandered around town. The streets were filled with people. From the shadows of the coffee shops came Western ballads and the intimate laughter of young lovers. It was harvest time. Hirosaki apples, cool and glistening in pyramids of four, filled a table under a string of oversized light bulbs. An abundant supply of hand-power had wrapped the apples in a newsprint bag since their first days as a blossom. Now these same hands washed and polished the fruit until they shone heavy red and succulent, polka-dotting the white saucers under them. Any one of fifty, set alongside the apple which gave to Snow White, would have given the poor girl a moment of indecision. I bought two, more for the privilege of breaking the polished red skin with my teeth than out of hunger.

The next morning, two hours out of Sendai, I had my first and only accident of the trip. Plunging down a hill, I ran into a curve and a new gravel bed at the same time. The curve was not sharp, but the tiny stones were packed almost five inches deep. My front wheel angled crazily, and I was suddenly on my side, sliding across the road. The cycle and I came to rest in a dry ditch. The fall snapped off my right foot pedal but outside of that, all was well. At the next town I stopped at a machine shop. With the approval (*I think*) of an old man who was the only occupant of the shop, I chopped off the top of one of his broom handles and inserted that for a support. It sufficed.

The road, indeed, the entire countryside, began to take on what I shall call, for want of a better term, an American air. There were billboards, announcements of Rotary Club luncheons, traffic lights and even traffic jams.

I first saw Tokyo in the shadows of a setting sun. It was not a pretty first sight. In rural areas, countries truly differ. In America, even within states, there are differences in styles of rural living. But cities everywhere must pay a price of uniformity for their industrial development. The steel mills of Gary, Indiana, the giant electric plants of Toshiba and General Electric all present the same façade from a distance. A smokestack is a smokestack the world over. And so is haze and industrial grayness.

An hour later I was racing along the ocean on the last lap home. From what little I had seen of it before the evening sky tinged its depths, it was a bluer and more feminine sea than Mutsu Bay. By now my standards had adjusted to those of Tokyo. The modern two-lane highway did not surprise me, nor did the gleaming toll booths and uniformed collectors with their ever-present pad of receipts. It was like the Merritt Parkway between Connecticut and New York.

And yet, even as I saw the much-heralded lights of Atami spread out before me and contemplated my new life in a place where it never snowed and no one ever froze to death on the sidewalks, I thought again of my horse-cart-crowded road up north. It was long past. I would never again have to take to a ditch or thinking about sliding under a horse. I would never write that sonnet, for the wonder of good roads would be lost in the daily use of them.

It was a wearying trip. Some parts were not deserving of the name, road. It was dirty, dusty; the signposts were rare, gas stations hard to find, spare parts were unavailable.

But times are changing. All along the way, men were digging and oiling the road. There is talk if a super-highway from Aomori to Kagoshima in Kyushu. Speeds of one hundred kilometers per hour are predicted. Fine. They will probably have billboards every kilometer of the way, correct signposts in English, French

Chapter 18

and German as well as Japanese, large gas stations selling Coca-Cola, perhaps a few *pachinko* parlors set up.

The day is coming. I am not one with the sentimental tourist disappointed because Japanese women no longer wear kimonos only. Drive the road through. But when you do, it will cost you something. When your highways flow in sterile, perfectly engineered concrete ribbons from Mutsu Bay to Kagoshima Bay, you will lose what the roads in America have lost, never to regain; what I found the nicest feature about cycling in Japan; namely a touch of challenge, a touch of romance and adventure.

And, when your super-highways become a reality, I will prefer to remember the Ōshū-Kaidō as it was in the summer of '60, when you had to dodge horse-carts and, huddled in your sleeping bag hearing twigs breaking in the rice fields, you were never altogether positive it was not mountain bandits stalking about in the mysterious star-filled Asiatic night.

19

Everyday Health on the College Campus

Save yourself — and the planet — by going to college! The college years are the optimal period for adults to learn and adopt healthy practices that can be a source of growth and personal development for a lifetime. From eating healthy to thinking healthy to living healthy, it turns out that college is the perfect time and place to learn about ways to live in better balance with yourself, your family, your culture, your romantic partner, your neighbor, your community, your workplace, and in positive coexistence with our planet. The current well-being trends on college campuses show that well-being of college students is not just a passing fad.

Many colleges and universities are adopting well-being practices, programs, and facilities that places student well-being on par with other mission-critical goals such as global citizenship, civic engagement, and the production of new knowledge. No longer is student well-being considered ancillary to the work of the institution of higher learning. Those working in student services and academic support in college leadership are taking responsibility for the health and well-being of the whole student, which underscores the importance of college life and ways it can shape choices for a lifetime. Working across academic and student services programs, these student well-being programs are changing how colleges and students view well-being.

In fact, the global mission of health and well-being on college campuses transcends student well-being and filters upstream to the staff, faculty, and the community. Healthy Campus Network (HCN) is a University of California system-wide initiative that promotes innovative reforms in all dimensions of health and well-being "to make UC the healthiest place to work, learn, and live" (Office of the President, 2018).

In the past, student health programs have focused on preventing high-risk behavior i.e., suicide, alcohol, drug use, smoking, sexual violence, hazing, eating disorders, and self-harm. In fact, there are new CAS national standards for preventing high-risk behaviors that are being developed currently. The prevention of high-risk behaviors makes up most programs and funding dedicated to health, and it is rightly so, yet new focus on student well-being provides hope for the promotion of healthy behaviors as well.

Taking advantage of current evidence-based research on psychology, neuroscience, human performance, and sustainability, these preventative student well-being measures are as helpful to the students as they are to the institutions themselves. Healthy students mean student success. Healthy campuses mean financial and environmental success.

Timing is everything and these days, colleges face an unusually vulnerable student population. With the pressure of the post-9/11 era and Covid-19 pandemic, cases of depression and anxiety are off the charts for the general population. As well, changes in technology use with the advent of smart phones and the proliferation of social media as well as the rising cost of higher education and an increase in high school shootings in the last 10 years, the #MeToo Movement and Black Lives Matter Movement, current college students are navigating a perfect storm of stress in an environment that is rife with pressure unlike any other generation in recent history.

The annual National College Health Assessment (NCHA) survey showed that a third of students have experienced emotional turmoil that affected their college participation. College students identified the top impediments to academic performance as anxiety and depression.

Chapter 19

Fortunately, colleges and university are stepping up to the challenge of addressing student well-being with gusto! Many of the nation's top colleges are instituting wellness programs along with academic research and studies into personal well-being.

In fact, student well-being support is now seen as a recruiting tool in luring students during the college search process. Not only do health programs address traditional concerns such as weight-loss, nutrition, and physical fitness, but they also address areas such as mental resilience, sustainability and social ecology, and financial well-being as all playing a role in stress reduction. From Harvard University to the College of William and Mary to the University of Oregon to University of Virginia, substantial research, funding, and facilities have been devoted to student well-being. A healthier college campus means a healthier student and a healthier planet.

Recent student health and well-being trends include the following:

Social and Personal Support Programs

Colleges are offering programs and peer support groups to support positive mental health and stress reduction i.e., resilience, kindness, healthy eating circles, personal identity support programs for LGBTQIA+, single parents, military veterans, low-income students, and first-generation support programs such as Umoja, Friend-to-Friend, and well-being protection programs such as Active Bystander Programs, and Peer Education on Early Alerts, and Finals Stress Reduction Programs.

Institutional Support Programs

Colleges are participating in and offering Health and Safety Hotlines, Early Alerts, Beyond Consent, Habitudes, Health Education Awareness Resource Teams, Healthy Campuses, 8 Dimensions of Wellness, Healthy Minds Study, MyPlate, College Farmer's Markets, Greenest College Rankings, and Restorative Justice.

Academic Programs in Health and Well-being

Colleges are offering college credit for health and well-being practices such as volunteering, interning, researching, and working in ways that benefit your health, community, and the planet. In addition, colleges are offering classes in Social Ecology, Positive Psychology, Stress Reduction, Mindfulness, Relaxation, and Self-care. Complete majors and degrees are offered at the Positive Psychology Center and my own major, holistic Health Education, and Environmental Sustainability. The human experience is gaining more attention due to Diversity Initiatives about inclusion and belonging across the curriculum. Colleges offer courses on Being Human in STEM to aid in the well-being of students of color in the sciences.

Join the party for student well-being on the college campus! While college is certainly a time of stress, pressure, and challenge, more and more colleges are stepping up to remove the stigma and shame that comes along with asking for assistance with stress, anxiety, and depression. As well the idea of well-being is growing to include not just physical health, but mind, body, spirit, and community. By making programs visible, welcoming, and accessible to all students, more students will develop and learn healthy habits that will continue to benefit them and our collective community.

Student health is not just about avoiding the Freshman 15. Now it is about developing healthy habits for a lifetime! So, ask for help, seek out support, and find out all the ways that you can be a healthy and happy college student and maybe save the world along the way!

20

Healthy Behavior Change

People may not agree with me, but I do not accept the belief that making a healthy change needs to be stressful. I disagree that changes in our health behavior needs to be big and scary, be it starting a new eating plan or setting new sleep goals or deciding to quit smoking. I reject the idea that the natural response to making a health behavior change is fear and opposition. Making a health behavior change need not be threatening to someone's sense of personal freedom. Instead making a health behavior change should be a return to a healthier version of yourself. That optimistic viewpoint can be difficult.

There is a troubling concept of the Immunity to Change centered on the idea that people sabotage positive health change and resist change like the body's immune system resistance to foreign substances in the body. Unfortunately, the current anti-vax resistance proves the Immunity to Change is very real and people are willing to die from a preventable disease rather than change their mind about taking a vaccine. Immunity to Change is deadly, even after over 800,000 deaths from Covid in 2022. Many people still resist taking a proven vaccine that would prevent transmission due to their personal beliefs and fears.

Still, I disagree that all people are instinctively opposed to change. After all that flies in the face of the concept I hold dear about continuous growth, *élan vital*. In fact, I feel that as humans we are much more than likely to be drawn to the bright, shiny, and new, novel, different, exotic, strange, usual, or unknown, in many instances.

When people experience a new way of life, like trying a

health behavior change, there is often a sense of loss of control. Yet psychologically there is also a natural stabilizing or adaptive phase, or allostasis that is part of the process to achieve homeostasis. Even so, there is often a yearning to return to "normal" or previous poor behavior. This yearning can be a desire to give up the health behavior change even though it is a positive change. This is the point when a person is in-between adopting a new health change and returning or backsliding to a previous unhealthy behavior. This "in-between" stage is when many people give up. The in-between stage or liminal period of allostasis is a necessary stage in development and in learning. Another way to view allostasis, is, that homeostasis is the pause between states of allostasis. Allostasis is also the period when many people should be asking for help!

Allostasis is necessary for transformation, but it need not be so negative. Just like when one is learning to walk or speak another language, people learn to accommodate and assimilate the new health behavior. This is when change is incorporated in the middle of transformation that leads to a new level of homeostasis or new level of stability in their sense of self and identity.

The idea that a person will automatically respond to transformation with rejection and sabotage is purely a matter of mental framing of the change and perception and based on "deficit-based thinking". There can be any number of responses to the notion of change. Attitude makes all the difference.

There are so many health changes that occur throughout a lifetime that our definition of health change needs to include transformation as a part of everyday life.

Everyday natural occurrences happen from growth and human development that are forms of health change. The human body goes through all kinds of changes that drastically transform and change our ideas about our sense of self and how we see ourselves, i.e. puberty, sexual identity and development, injuries, illness, trauma, social status, menopause, pregnancy, physical development and abilities, aging, etc.

What is believed to be a static state is never long-lasting, just as states of allostasis are short-lived. What is needed is the ability to emotionally regulate and anticipate change as a natural state of being alive, just as our physical bodies must regulate itself during these times of change.

I understand the perceived fear about health behavior change is in the subconscious and below our level of awareness. Yet our perception can be developed to understand how it is affected by our feelings, thoughts, and most importantly our attitude.

There is abundant research on the influence of our attitude on mind body health and in the importance of faith in self-healing. It is important to include resistance to the concept of the body's ability to heal itself in the understanding of the Immunity to Change response.

There is tremendous benefit to learning about the role of resistance and opposition to change in health, but I do not believe that people are predisposed to view health behavior change with opposition.

Transformation is not about a negative or a positive that should be perceived as a threat to personal freedom or as a harm to our sense of self, it is simply a change process.

Does the perception of health change have to be so negative?

Why is the common belief that health behavior change must be difficult and that it is natural to resist health change?

Is the Immunity to Change a real threat to making lasting heath behavior change?

I do not believe that is the case for most people. Unfortunately, during the Covid-19 pandemic, the Immunity to Change at the societal level is a real threat for some communities and it is prolonging the recovery from the pandemic for everyone else.

People talk about being a "work in progress" or refer to being on "a journey" to being the "best version" of their selves. Just looking at the many stages of human development and in learning about the brain's neuroplasticity, epigenetics, and the microbiome, change and transformation is constantly happening on the molecular, conscious, and subconscious levels.

While homeostasis is the state of being stable, it is just as important to understand about allostasis and the process of adaption. Our sense of identity and our physical bodies are not a static thing or constant, because there are always new experiences, feelings, connections, relations, and interactions that happen daily to destabilize the living environment, and our sense of self or what we know to be our sense of self must change with it.

Part of living to a ripe old age, is the ability to process information one is exposed to so one can learn to use and incorporate information for personal growth and development or in making sense of the world.

The realization that life changes and growth are our natural state of being is like the belief of being a lifelong learner. Once a person is open to being a student for life, life opens with endless possibilities, learning, and change opportunities!

Learning in life never ends. Learning is change and learning is transformation. Just as one never stops learning, one never stops changing.

If we work from the premise that all people are naturally predisposed to favor the state of homeostasis and stability, we lose sight of the fact that change is all around, and homeostasis includes opportunity and space for change to happen. Thus, it can be that there can be people just as predisposed to favor liminal space and allostasis as there are people who resist.

If a person is threatened by health behavior change, that is something that is personal and not universal.

Does it happen, this Immunity to Change? Of course, but it does not have to be that way. I believe, every person can change their lives if they make a positive intention to do so.

Every single person can change because we all have the power to change our attitude!

Part III

Nurturing Our Self During the Job Search

21

Rugged Individualism is a Myth

When I was in 5th grade at Woodcrest Elementary in the City of Fullerton, we played this computer game called Oregon Trail. I was in 5th grade in 1985, so using computers was all the rage in elementary schools across California.

Oregon Trail had heavily pixelated graphics on a black and green screen. The game was a life simulation game about completing the Oregon Trail during the westward expansion of the United States. A family would need to plan out food rations, routes to take, the care of animals, and protection from sickness and danger. You could lose your food rations, children would get sick and die, and the oxen would drown in the river. All manners of disaster would befall the intrepid party on the way to Oregon. There were trials and tribulations, but the party was determined to move on to the ultimate destination and always kept making progress. The game would encourage the players to press on. Always forward. Onward and Upward!

Recently my 14-year-old son came home and told me he was playing Oregon Trail in his eight-grade class in middle school. I asked him about his provisions and if anyone had gotten ill from dysentery. The circle of life continues.

The game of Oregon Trail shows us the power of persistence and determination. To always press on. Onward and Upward.

As adults, we know there are many times in life when we wonder if the journey is worth taking. Is the cost of taking the journey really going to pay off in the end? When these kinds of doubts enter your thinking, this is when you need to find your inner strength.

We all face doubts, second guessing ourselves, willing ourselves to give up. It is so tempting to give up. The allure of quitting is always present. Especially when it feels as if all hope is lost. It is when you feel at your lowest point that you must seek out help the most. We cannot allow the fear of failure prevent us from seeking out support along the way!

While the Oregon Trail harkens back to a time of self-reliance and idealized rugged individualism steeped in Americana tradition, it presents a false narrative of survival and the pioneer experience that should be taken with a grain of salt.

We are not alone on the trail of life, no one is! We live in a society of relationships, connections, communities, and likeminded peers seeking out journeys like our own.

While I appreciate the disaster-prone simulation game because it brings back nostalgia for a simpler time in my own upbringing, I now realize the importance of context, community, and relationships in the success of one's life journey.

Perhaps a more realistic tenet is the old African proverb, "If you want to go fast, go alone: if you want to go far, go together."

Determination and persistence may help one move onward and upward, but life's journey is infinitely better when we work together, with our family, friends, communities, and as a collective to make it to the destination. So, let's press onward and upward, together!

22

Personal Bias Can be Transcended

Racism, classism, sexism, heterosexism, cissexism, xenophobia, homo/transphobia, nationalism, religiosity, and many socially constructed ideas come from places of fear and the natural behavior of groups of people as they attempt to make sense in a senseless world. Interestingly, even at times of peak animosity and division, human safety and survival trumps over hate and fear. Anyone can empirically observe the humanity and charity pouring in to support the people of Houston to affirm that there truly is goodness in the world, no matter our perceived differences.

Summer 2017 could have easily gone down in history as a turning point in our nation's civil rights history as a time when inciting hate, bigotry, violence became socially accepted by our national and local leaders in government. There were rumblings that "both sides" had valid points when it came to intolerance, finger-pointing, destruction, fearmongering, strong-arming, bullying, and criminal behaviors. Threats to free speech and personal freedoms were being tossed around by both sides like grenades to prove points that no longer seemed to consider that most people have biases and experiences that fall closer to the middle ground than to the extreme left or right of either argument.

Fact is, personal bias is a survival mechanism and works, often, to bring communities of people together for survival and safety more so than it does for war and violence. Below is the Pyramid of Hate that shows how hate can escalate.

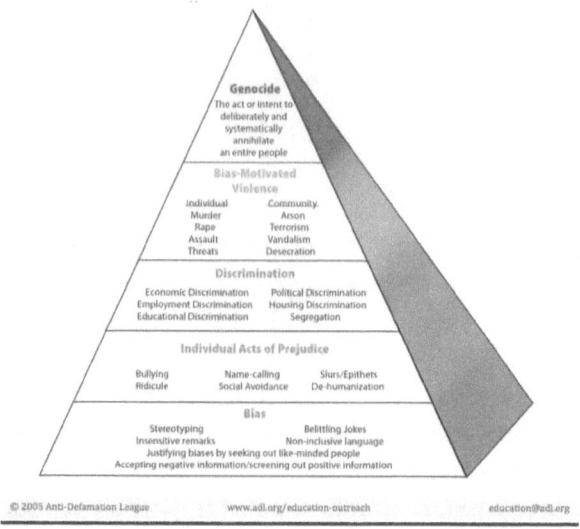

While words like racist, sexist, and others get a big reaction in ugly debates, the fact is that there is a spectrum of hate. Not all white people are racists, but all people, no matter their skin tone/color, do have personal biases.

The good news is that we can overcome our personal biases. It is an active choice we can all make as thinking humans. Look at the people of Houston, Texas. Neighbors helping neighbors. Black people helping white people. Poor people helping rich people. Spanish-speaking people helping English-speaking people. Recent immigrants helping native-born citizens. Mexico helping the United States. A hurricane named Harvey has restored my faith in humanity. The people of Texas show that though we are tested by disaster, the spirit remains!

https://implicit.harvard.edu/implicit/takeatest.html

To learn more about your bias, here is the implicit bias test available at the link above. Every person should explore and learn about their own biases.

I have taken all the various implicit bias tests. I have learned to understand and identify my own biases. With that in mind, I consciously choose to work on this for my own personal development. Here are some things that I do to eradicate my own ignorance when it comes to cultural diversity:

1. Learn about cultures/histories other than my own
2. Communicate with all people in a respectful manner by the way I listen, speak, and act
3. Value contributions to the community and society by all its members
4. Encourage the expression of multiple voices/ viewpoints/ perspectives in the community

What are some steps that you take to eradicate your personal biases?

We cannot let our sense of pride and prejudice affect our sense of humanity. I firmly believe that together we can all take steps each day to eradicate our own ignorance, to live better, richer, more meaningful lives. But that is my own personal bias.

23

Life Transitions are Times of Community Nurturing

Last week I attended a funeral. It was not a funeral for somebody I knew personally. The funeral was for the adult daughter of someone I used to work with a few years ago. I was the former supervisor of the father of the deceased. He was someone whom I had worked with on a regular basis in my former position. I knew he was getting older and came from a small family. This loss meant he now had very few living relatives left. Anytime someone experiences a loss it is terrible, but especially when it is a son or daughter, it is difficult to imagine. What a tragedy!

I knew that attending the funeral service meant I would cross paths with other former colleagues. I could have chosen to stay away, but I was earnestly interested in offering my condolences to my former colleague. What made it difficult for me to make the determination of whether to attend was since my leaving my previous position was not under the best of terms. In fact, there were several people who told me under strictest confidence that some staff lobbied for the eradication of my position. Still, in the greater scheme of things, I felt it was important for me to appear.

I weighed the pros and cons. I am not the type of person who allows other people's perception of me to determine my self-worth. I respect that people have perspectives and viewpoints different than my own. As well everyone is entitled to their own opinion. I know that there were times when I made unpopular decisions and there were times when I was not swayed by certain people in my area that had opinions that were clearly self-serving. I stand behind my actions. I know that I take my responsibilities to always act with the best interest of the organization. I knew I might be uncomfortable to be in the presence of my dissenters, but I felt it was more important to show emotional support to someone in his time of need.

When we manage groups of people, our relationships can be strained and stained by decisions we make as leaders. But there should never be a time when we lose our sense of humanity. How can we approach sensitive gatherings when you leave your last position on a sour note?

Be genuine

I wanted to extend my sincere condolences. There was no other hidden agenda or purpose for my visit other than to express my sympathies. Someone who is facing a loss does not need people there to take advantage of a funeral to make a point. If you are not there to express your honest emotions, then maybe it is not the place for you.

Be generous

Funerals and weddings and births are all symbolic life occurrences. There are often religious expressions and practices. It is a wonderful way to join in a shared experience for a group to remember, rejoice, and revel in the passing of time of a person into their new plane of existence. Being open to new rituals and methods of processing emotions shows you more about other people's way of life.

Be gregarious

The gathering of people to remember a loved one is about being together and sharing thoughts. Everyone is a friend when you are struggling to understand the meaning of something that doesn't make any sense. It is a time to share stories and memories and feelings. There were a few famous people who passed away last week. It can be very cathartic to process loss with other people who are experiencing loss together.

Be gentle

Everyone goes through the experiences of dealing with loss of a loved one at one point or another. It is the human condition. Our relationship with our colleagues can be personal or professional but it is important to express joy and sympathy. While some work relationships are closer than others, not every person handles grief the same. It is important to be gentle with yourself and others. Funerals bring up memories, recollections, and feelings that can surprise you. It is important to check your own feelings to determine if you have enough emotional control for a social situation.

Coming together for times of celebration and grief are important rituals that define our society. We can benefit by reminding ourselves that emotions do serve a purpose in the workplace. Emotions connect us to our roles and the people with whom we work. In times of joy and sorrow, it should not be gauche to show you care. At the end of the day, it is our personal relationships that matter most.

24

Getting Sidetracked is Par for the Course

Everyone talks about pursuing your passion. Following your heart. Taking the right steps to land your "dream job". But what happens if your dream job NEVER shows up?

Some of us have worked, sacrificed, engineered, planned, strategized, and pursued a very specific career path. We may have completed education, internships, work experience, and industry specific training to work in this field. We know exactly what we want to do and how to do it. Perhaps we have stepped onto the career path and fell off for some reason. We already know the dream job is out there. We simply need to get it.

In the meantime, we take a sidetrack job. This job is something we take because it relates somewhat to the job of our dreams. Perhaps we are working in a field, location, industry, area that serves the same population, purpose, or teaches you about a related industry, or is a partner in the field you really prefer working.

There is value in the sidetrack job.

We have all been there. Working a job that is not our passion, but it pays the bills. What can one do if they are stuck in a sidetrack job?

Learn, learn, and learn!
With the availability of information increasing exponentially over time, we all must commit to being lifelong learners. As well, we must learn to understand what is pertinent and meaningful to our work and the community we wish to serve. Working a

sidetrack job allows you to explore, discover, learn, experiment, and understand a whole new area of your community. Learn about industry practices, partners, gaps in service, and opportunities for growth, organizational priorities, and new ways of doing business. Each organization has a method of working, each industry has a focus and value that is unique. Here is a chance to learn skills, competencies, and technologies new to you. As well, taking a sidetrack job is a wonderful way to use your professional skills in a whole new way!

Staying is up to you!
How long does one stay in a sidetrack job? Depending on the amount of learning taking place, it may make sense to stay a while. Learn as much as you can before moving on to your next venture. You may never have this opportunity to be in that type of industry again. You may even find out that it makes better sense to stay indefinitely. Perhaps this is a new dream job that you never envisioned. On the other hand, you might feel like it is a total mismatch and the shorter the time frame the better. Especially if the position is outside your field, staying less than 6 months could make total sense.

Go with the Flow
It is human habit to compare the old with the new. You might find yourself biting your tongue about policies, practices, methods, and protocols that you are familiar with from your previous industry. But different places do business in different ways. Often there is precedent, law, traditional reasons that you would not know as a new member to the organization. Look around and observe the organizational culture and practices to help in the transition.

Don't Give Up!
Some people who find themselves on the outside looking in

can lose hope. It can be easy to feel like you will never get back to where you used to be before. Have patience and faith! You were there before because you have what it takes. It might feel like your dream job quit you. I have heard tales of people who spent 10 years to finally land their dream job! They never gave up. You must never give up!

Stay Connected!

There are always changes in the industry. New laws, legislation, technologies, competencies, focus, challenges, threats, developments, skills, and expectations. You must stay current on what is happening in your field. Just as you would if you were working in your dream job. You need to stay on top of current trends. Read industry publications, attend conferences, network with industry leaders, keep current on potential employers. Most importantly, keep a solid connection with former employers and supervisors. After all, these will be your references when you get that next interview!

Re-imagine a New Dream Job

Perhaps your original motivation to pursue a dream job was based on helping others. There are countless organizations and industries that focus on helping others. It can be easy to think of only one, true-blue dream job. But why not imagine a few dream jobs? There could be dream jobs in a variety of industries. For example, perhaps you enjoy outreach, working with the public and informing them about your organization. There are many, many careers that could be described this way from human resources to marketing to sales to healthcare. It is really about how you frame it in your own mind that makes it meaningful to you. Don't fall into the trap of thinking you can only work for a particular industry or brand name organization to be happy. Why limit yourself that way?

The sidetrack job can sometimes feel like a waste of time. But as they say, time is an illusion. And if you waste your time or not, it is all up to you to decide. Either way it is important to never take the sidetrack job for granted. After all, it is part of your life's journey. It might lead your life in a completely new direction that you never even saw coming! Might as well enjoy the ride.

25

Look Back and Forward in Gratitud*e*

The year started out with a marriage proposal, and it was all downhill from there. What can top that kind of event in terms of the emotional excitement?

Well, to be fair, this so-called marriage proposal came from someone I had not seen in over 2 years. It was not exactly from someone I would consider a potential suitor in any sense of the word. Plus, I am not sure an email proposal that was in my spam folder counts. But what the proposal did was make me think about my dreams, goals, expectations, ambitions, pie-in-the-sky wishes – what I wanted out of life and what I was doing about it!

As any reflective professional in leadership has done in their moments of stillness and calm, I contemplate life goals. What DO I really want to do and what is yet to be accomplished?

When students graduate from high school or college there is a book that is often given as a gift to celebrate this important milestone. The book is "Oh, the Places You'll Go" by Dr. Seuss. It talks about the future as this mystical amazing place that is out there - a place to go! It is a book that harkens back to a time of wonderment and fascination in the possible. It is full of honesty and charm.

We need to keep that momentum and hope for the future going! We all need to be reminded of the wonderful potential in all of us and in the world, especially when life feels like everything is topsy-turvy.

All amazing things have a beginning, middle, and end. This year has been an important wake up call to pay attention to the places in my life that are dull, monotonous, and out of sync. Why is a marriage proposal exciting? It is because it is an opportunity to start on a new path. To build a new life. To begin anew with a partner for life.

What is missing in your life is just as important as what is in your life. It helps you to think about your next direction and your next step. Where do you want to go and who do you want to be there?

As I think about this year being almost half over, I reflect on what I want to accomplish in my life.

I do know what I really want to do, and I know what is yet to be accomplished. I know this because I know myself. And that is something that I did not have when I graduated from college or high school. It is something I have learned over time and through my various life experiences. And, Oh, the places I have been!

26

Prove Yourself Even in the Small Roles

In the last 4 months I have worked at 6 different jobs. I have been a limousine driver, substitute teacher, outbound sales representative, data entry clerk, wine tour driver, and elections committee clerk. Since I have been out of work for almost 2 years, I basically felt the need to earn a paycheck by any means necessary.

Being unemployed is not *that* unusual. Being unemployed for a few months is not *that* unusual. But being unemployed for 2 years when you have a doctorate degree and 15 years' experience in a professional field with no termination for cause or failure to complete a probationary period or request for voluntary discharge, no previous gaps in employment history, and a spotless criminal record is a little more unusual.

Something else unusual, in the last 2 years I have interviewed for over 50 positions, and I was a final candidate over 20 times. Yet, after all that effort, not one, single job offer to show for it. TOTAL REJECTION!

So, I decided to think outside the box. I needed to find a way to support my family. It was time to bite the bullet. Time to look anywhere and everywhere. There is NO SHAME in doing what gots to be done!

Over the last 4 months, I have had some interesting experiences. I must admit that in a few instances, I was kinda having some fun working these odd jobs. I was doing things I haven't done in years, like working in customer service, data entry, sales, and teaching. It felt good helping with the primary elections during this tumultuous election cycle. I also got experience as a substitute teacher at various middle schools and high schools. And it was pretty special driving groups around the Napa Valley on wine tours and to concerts in Oakland.

Yet, on the day I began the job as a driver, I felt like that old cliché of the taxi driver with a doctorate. So humiliating! One day I was sitting in my limousine waiting for the passengers who were at a nearby restaurant on the waterfront. An elderly lady out for an evening stroll saw me sitting in the car. She approached me and asked me if I was the driver of this stretched out sedan. I said, "Yes". This perfect stranger was simply thrilled that I was the driver! You could tell that she got a kick out of the idea that I was driving a limousine. She was so psyched that it was contagious. Before the lady went on her way, she gave me a high five. All of a sudden it seemed kinda cool to be driving a limo. I felt like I was tearing down a wall of gender segregation in the workplace. I was a pioneer! This friendly lady made my day and I made hers!

Another time, I was working at a call center as a sales rep. I was being trained by a young man who was about 20 years old. He was explaining how to build rapport with customers. After his training he watched me take some calls with actual customers. He said I was really good at speaking with people. The young man asked me about my past work experience. I explained I had 15 years' experience working in higher education. We got to talking about college. The guy said he was always interested in going to college for business. I explained that there are classes he can take at the college right down the road! The young man decided to learn more about the local college after talking about it with me. Before I left that job assignment, he said he was enrolled at the local college for the next semester. Maybe I put that man on a road to a college degree and a whole new opportunity for him and his family.

Then a few weeks ago, I finally managed to land a full-time position. Hallelujah!

Chapter 26

The search is finally over for now!

As I think about the last few months, I realize, while we might feel the need to get that paycheck by any means necessary, it is important to never forget that you can have fun and enjoy yourself along the way. We are all working to provide for our family and our community, but we can make a positive impact no matter what job we might have at the moment.

I am grateful for the chance people took on me while I was looking for a permanent position. These experiences will no doubt shape the leader I am and the relationships I will have with my staff.

These life experiences, no matter how big or small, make us unique.

There is a quote that has always stood out to me about our roles in life. "There are no small parts, only small actors" by Constantin Stanislavski.

I say, "There is no such thing as a small job. Every job is an opportunity to prove yourself to the world."

Go out there and make a difference!

27

Passion Projects Rock

Have you ever worked on a project that felt like a dream project? You had the right resources, support, vision, participation, budget, knowledge, just about EVERYTHING about it was perfect!

Even after the project came and went, the mere thought about the project brings a smile to your face.

That was your JAM!

Good times! The best of times!

There are many instances I can recall where I felt a sense of flow during a passion project, like everything was coming together perfectly, effortlessly, and miraculously. These kinds of experiences at work are the positive outcomes of a healthy, productive work environment.

As well, it takes a personal mindset about work that flow is possible and natural. In my eyes, there needs to be a confluence of personality, environment, and actions that allow states of flow to happen at work.

So how can we manifest flow and engineer positive outcomes at work? I believe it all comes down to identifying and recognizing passion projects.

How is a passion project defined? What is the role of management and staff in identifying and determining participation in a passion project? Does a passion project come from the top down or from the ground up?

You will be annoyed by the answers to these questions, but the answer is......it depends!

"Ugh, c'mon!" you might be thinking...

Well, it is true. Passion is subjective and different people perceive the same thing a million different ways. In the end, it is all about the human experience.

Below I will list a few key elements that stood out from passion projects in my past:

There is alignment of personal values and interests with professional training, skills, abilities

You have this inexplicable feeling of extreme competence doing the necessary tasks for the project. It feels like your whole work life has led up to your role in this assignment.

Your work energizes and uplifts your spirit

There is a feeling of excitement and pride in your work. You look forward to spending time on the project and taking on responsibilities with gusto. You wish there were more hours in the day because you feed off the energy of working on the project. Your name is all over it and you cannot wait to share it with others.

There is an endpoint to the project

While you feel 100% alive working on the assignment, part of the joy comes from knowing it will soon end. You give your full attention to the details because you know it will all be over. The project may go on in a different phase or under different leadership, but you are not responsible ad infinitum.

The work embodies the organization's core mission and purpose

Support for the project falls right in line with everything everybody is always talking about. Your value proposition is exactly what the project is all about. It hits the nail on the head! And everybody knows it!

Chapter 27

It wasn't love at first sight; it was a fixer upper

A project does not start out all fine-tuned and pre-packaged to be a passion project. A project develops into a passion project. I doubt you can buy a passion project right off the rack. It takes input, tweaking, and doing those finishing touches for it to be a true passion project. That personal touch depends on the person and the organization. It is all about attitude.

It sets a new standard of excellence

After completing a passion project, your skills, abilities, and knowledge are stretched and further developed in new and interesting ways. Perhaps you did something new for the first time or acquired new knowledge in order to be successful. Either way a passion project raises your notion of a personal best. It can help establish peaks in your professional development.

Everyone should have the opportunity and access to passion projects. From the entry level recent college graduate to the most seasoned veteran. It helps people feel motivated and reminds staff of their value as professionals in the organization.

28

Making Space for Professional Loyalty

Stick and stones may break my bones, but words will never hurt me. This used to be an innocent saying. It used to make sense that words could be ignored, or their power deflected through mental fortitude. This is not the case in today's world.

These days the power of words cannot be underestimated. Especially in today's uber-sensitive landscape of social media. A single poorly phrased tweet can sink reputations faster than the most genuine and perfectly worded apology. A Facebook post can mean the end of your career. An online comment can spread faster than wildfire on a hot summer day in the middle of a California drought.

But I want to address the power of words on the micro level, in the day-to-day interactions and comments made in the course of an average day.

The power of what we say has a direct impact on the culture we create in our organizations and on the perception of our organization out in the communities we serve. As managers we serve the role of representing our institutions at the most basic level. After all, in a sense, we are the institution!

Recently I was attending an employee orientation and was struck by something that I thought was a positive practice that I want to bring to your attention.

There was a point in the orientation where a statement was read about the importance of loyalty and pride in the staff of the organization. It said "individual criticism of another educator or other schools destroys public faith in all educators and schools.

Nothing else so feeds the fires of public distrust. Particularly desirable is loyalty to the public school system and community. Gossip from school is inexcusable. Loyalty to the profession is next after pride for effective educator public relations. Where praise seems impossible, silence is the rule."

Huh?

At first, my critical thinking mind was aghast! How dare this institution assume I would assign my loyalty to an organization where criticism was not publicly and openly discussed? I have believed that critical inquiry demanded public discourse in order to achieve and promote democratic inclusivity.

But then I thought more deeply about the message. "Individual criticism" stood out as well as "loyalty to the profession". I felt like I was having a crisis of faith but then there was a moment of clarity!

I was not really suffering a crisis of faith. I was experiencing a moment of personal growth and understanding.

Of course!

Criticism is important to organizational development, but there is a time and a place. As well, loyalty to the profession means avowing to defend the institution from harm or criticism.

Part of our responsibility as agents within an organization is to defend against those perceptions that damage the reputation of the organization.

These are ideals I have always held but the language was never articulated in such a fashion.

What an important lesson!

Another issue I realized caused me to initially question these notions, were the experiences I had where my fellow managers and leadership failed to demonstrate professional loyalty and pride. This does happen and will occur in the future. Nobody is perfect. We all stick our foot in our mouth at some point.

But with this realization, I can now pinpoint my discomfort. I can now recognize that I have a high level of loyalty and pride for public education. That does not mean everyone share's those values. But it is something that is important to me.

Disparaging comments made about an organization lead to a toxic environment. At the same time, conversations must take place to address problems and areas of improvement. The deal breaker between a toxic and healthy environment rests on the amount of respect and trust there is between the organization and the employees.

Respect breeds respect. The most uncomfortable topic can be addressed as long as it comes from a place of respect.

Criticism does not have to be confrontational. As well, loyalty does not have to be blind. Only through honest conversations can organizations see real improvement.

There needs to be more discussion about professional loyalty and pride in the workplace.

Especially in the field of public education, where we have so many areas of improvement.

But we will not get there by throwing our institutions under the bus.

While there are places for improvement at every school, there are also a lot of places where there is some amazing work happening! So, let's see some pride here!

Our words do have power. Everyday conversations are important. Comments we make to each other and to others can do wonders to lift us up or tear us down.

Let's think twice about the power of our words. And let's show some professional loyalty and pride!

29

Road House Rules

The 1989 movie Road House is a cult classic for several reasons. But one aspect I want to draw attention to is the amount of badass leadership on display by the movie's protagonist Dalton, played by the one and only Patrick Swayze. This movie offers many examples that leaders can draw from to bring out their inner badass.

The movie premise is relatable enough for a study of leadership. "A tough bouncer is hired to tame a dirty bar." This short sentence is the deceptively simple synopsis provided on IMBD. But the movie is so much more than that. It is really a study in being a badass leader.

I will use some quotes from the movie to highlight ways everyone can be a badass leader at work.

"I run the show completely. When the job is done, I walk."

Dalton says this line when he is considering taking on the job for the first time. This line demonstrates the complete ownership that Dalton is willing to take on as a badass leader. He gives the job his 100% attention and effort, no questions asked. At the same time, Dalton knows his worth and he will leave when he feels the job is done. Being a badass leader means giving your all and then moving on to the next challenge when the time is right.

"I'm telling you straight. It's either my way or the highway."

Dalton holds a staff meeting on his first night at the bar.

During the staff meeting he lets half the team go for various misdeeds, including drug dealing, being rude, and general untrustworthiness. He makes this statement to show the staff that he is not messing around as a leader. He also demonstrates his expectations, standards, and intolerance for unethical behavior. Badass leaders make their expectations clear. Badass leaders walk the walk and talk the talk, so to speak.

"Always be nice."

Dalton is not a rough and tumble leader. He is a gentleman and genuinely considerate of others. He uses this line to teach the staff how to handle rude customers. Even in situations where it seems that everyone is getting ugly and rude, Dalton insists on being nice. A true badass leader makes those around them feel good about themselves, despite how ugly others may act to get their way.

"It's a job. It is nothing personal."

Dalton knows that there are times when people will say or do anything simply to get a rise out of you. Especially in his environment, people try to elicit a response that will likely lead to physical altercations. His strategy is to always expect the worst and be prepared for the best. But above all, do not take anything someone says as personal. A true badass leader knows that the job is to get the work done, not to take anything personal.

"It'll get worse before it gets better."

Dalton has experience of walking into the worst situations and turning them around. In fact, he is only called upon when times are at their worst. Places where there is no hope. He is not only a master of fixing places, but he knows that it is a long process that is not always smooth sailing. He keeps his cool. A badass leader has the confidence to weather the bad to get to the good. He does not give up!

Chapter 29

"It's amazing what you can get used to."

Dalton has seen it all. Others would see the same situation and call it a completely hopeless situation. He brings optimism and know-how and determination to his situation. You would not know what is possible unless you put yourself in new and challenging situations. The newer challenges you face, the easier it becomes to handle stressful situations. You get used to facing the impossible. The true badass leader can deal with the impossible and see the possible. Optimism is what makes the possible a reality.

Perhaps the best example of badass leadership is the end of the movie. Spoiler alert: Dalton does not kill the bad guy. But Dalton's badass leadership makes it possible for the townsfolk to develop their own inner badasses. Thus, the end is an example of how being a true badass leader means helping others turn into badass leaders themselves. Win/win!

While the rough and tumble cult classic movie Road House is not a traditional resource on how to be a badass leader, there are arguable some juicy tidbits that make watching the movie even more enjoyable when you see it as a lesson in leadership. It is fun to get inspiration from unusual sources.

30

Nope, Enough Ain't Enough

During any job search, there are many questions a person might ask of one's self. Should I apply for the job? Do I meet the qualifications based off the job description? Do I have the potential to be successful in the position? Are my credentials competitive compared to others who might be applying for the same position? Do I have a satisfactory combination of experience and skills? Would I be able to handle the workload of the new position? Would I be satisfied in the position? Is taking a new position the best decision for me and my family? Is the job a step up, down, lateral, or to fill a gap for a professional repertoire? Do I want to work for that specific institution/organization? What are the benefits and/or pitfalls of taking on a new job? How strong are my personal references?

Everyone goes through a critical personal assessment during a job search. We analyze our skills, education, experience, training, knowledge, shortcomings, achievements, and accomplishments. We wonder, ponder, explore, and worry about our likelihood of landing an interview. Depending on our state of mind, we can be our own best friend or our own worst enemy. We can lift ourselves up or tear ourselves down. So, how do we know when enough is enough? What do we do if we lost our motivation in our job search?

It takes energy, focus, enthusiasm, and creativity to conduct a job search. There are hours and hours of unpaid work scouring the job listings, applying for jobs, going on countless interviews, composing endless thank you emails, and answering question after question from friends and family about the job search.

It is no wonder that people often keep their job search to themselves. It is a long, drawn-out process. So, what is a person to do to maintain their sanity during a time of emotional highs and lows?

Friends, friends, friends!

We all have different kinds of friends. Some are superficial, surface-only friends. Some are fair-weather friends. Some are former-colleagues-turned friends. Some are known-forever-since-childhood friends. Some are ride-and-die friends. Some are been-through-hell-and-back-with-you friends. When the going gets tough, now is the time to get some true blue, ride-and-die friends. You need to surround yourself with real friends who you can count on to really listen and be supportive. Reevaluate the people you spend time with and cut out emotional vampires. True friends care, listen, follow up, and want to see you happy. Those people are your real friends. Let your friends know how they can help. They will be glad to be there for you!

Party Time!

Everyone needs to let off a little steam. There is no reason why you must be all serious in your job search all the time. A job search is stressful. Find time to party, dance, laugh, and let loose! Even if you can only take a few minutes to open a bottle of wine and enjoy a glass at the end of a long day. Relish the pure joy of taking a moment to relax. Make a ritual of taking time to unwind, be silly, tell jokes, sing songs, twirl around on the beach, take a walk in the park, and dance to some music! When you spend so much time concentrating on your search, you need to build in time for a release. Have fun every once in the while. It will recharge your batteries, which will help you have the energy to make your application even better the next time you apply!

Shake it Up!

A job search can fall into a routine, pattern, or rut. You check the same job listings, same websites, and same types of positions. It can become boring, monotonous, and tedious. Shake up your routine. Take time to apply for jobs that are completely outside the norm for someone of your background. Apply for positions that are right outside your skill set or in an organization/institution that seems like a stretch. Try to consider unconventional positions that may not be your first choice but match your skills and knowledge. If anything, you will learn something new about positions in different industries.

Choose a New Challenge!

The job search is a challenge, but it is important to have other life goals besides simply landing a new job. It can be hard to see beyond the immediate need of finding a new job, but it can be disheartening living day in and day out without seeing any personal progress and/or success. Set small and reachable goals so you can have some other potential areas of success in your life. Do you have fitness, financial, personal relationship, spiritual, lifestyle, or emotional goals that you can set as a challenge? Sure, you do! We all do! Maybe your goal is to learn a new skill or earn a certificate or gain a new hobby. You may not have control over the job search, but you certainly have control over the everyday decisions you make in your life. Choose a challenge that you can reach. Having success in your life will help you stay motivated and feel good about yourself!

Be Relentless!

Job satisfaction does not come easy. True leaders are always on a job search. Leaders are always on the hunt for a new skill, experience, or ability. Just as well, many people are on a job search because of looking for greener pastures and some are job seeking as a result of downsizing, re-organization, budget cuts, and reductions in force. There are many people on the job search through no fault of their own or circumstances outside their control such as a company going bankrupt, change in ownership, or other organizational upheaval. Whatever reason ignited the job search, to be successful you must be relentless. You can never give up. The job search is one job you can never quit! The sooner you resolve yourself to the need to be relentless the better. By reminding yourself that your will is strong, you will remember what led you to the search in the first place. You must be relentless in your sense of purpose, or you will lose motivation to keep going!

Unfortunately, there is no saying, "Enough is enough" when you are on the job search. Even more so, in life, there should be no saying, "Enough is enough". Especially when it comes to striving toward life satisfaction. I strive to live my life to the fullest, even while on the job search. So, yes, the job search continues for now. I will eventually find a position that is a good match. But more importantly, I will continue to find ways to make my life full and satisfying with or without a job to define my sense of personal satisfaction.

There was a riddle I remember from when I was a little girl. It goes, "What is the biggest room in the world?" The answer is, "The Room for Improvement". I have remembered this riddle all my life. It reminds me of the power we all have to improve our life.

31

Snowball's Chance in Hell

I knew I had a snowball's chance in hell of getting an interview. The position listed several key qualifications that I simply did not possess. Qualifications such as a specific graduate degree, certifications, licenses, and minimum years of experience that I did not have, yet I figured I would try my chances. It was a reach position.

I decided to go for it and send in my application anyway.

When I got invited for an interview, I was honestly perplexed. How did my application make it through the screening process? I was missing not one but a few of the minimum qualifications, how could I be invited for a campus interview?

I have been on hiring committees before as a hiring manager. I understand that minimum qualifications can be substituted for years of direct experience in a similar position. Committees occasionally waive certain requirements if the hiring pool is especially thin. But this is highly unusual. In this situation, it seems the pool barely qualified as a puddle.

I guess my 7 years of management experience was enough to suffice. I was thrilled to be given such consideration.

Of course, there are other reasons why candidates are sometimes considered for positions when they do not meet the minimum qualifications at first glance. One major reason is to get the candidate pool to meet certain "diversity requirements" determined by HR. Hiring committees in public agencies must meet diversity requirements in the makeup of the hiring committee as well as in the candidate pool. What does this mean? It means HR departments look at the race, gender, and other diversity elements of both the hiring committee and the candidate pool in the hiring process.

Knowing this, I always wonder if I am being asked to interview for a position simply to improve the diversity of the candidate pool. After all, I have a Latino sounding surname, I am a female in management, and I list a few ethnically focused professional associations/memberships on my resume. Plus I have a graduate degree from an Ivy League school and a doctorate that qualifies me for many different types of management positions. Lastly, I have direct experience in leading diversity initiatives and equity reporting experience. I make the perfect diversity candidate. For these reasons, I am not oblivious to the fact that I might be asked to interview as a diversity candidate.

Even still, I always go into an interview to get the job offer, whatever the circumstances. In addition, when I apply for a position, I honestly, and truly believe that I am the best candidate for the job. I would not apply for the job if I did not believe I could DO the job.

So, when the day of the interview arrived, I immediately noticed the diversity of the committee. I was especially pleased to see the committee included a student. It is always great to see a student on the hiring committee since I work in the field of higher education. I value an institution that goes the extra mile to include a student's voice in the hiring process. It demonstrates the importance the institution places on student input. I hold a similar value; my professional motto is *Students First!*

As the interview progressed, I did my best to show the connection between my experience, potential, and the job qualifications. I went into my usual spiel about my life story as a former community college student, how I am a single mother, how I was the first in my family to achieve my doctorate and how all this influences the daily decisions I would make as a person in this leadership position.

The interview was grueling and included an on-site writing

exercise which required me to address how recent state legislation would impact the institution's decision to transition from general funding to a basic aid budget funding model. I did my best, though I did feel like I was in over my head a little bit.

After the interview, I decided to take a walk around the campus. I wandered around the grounds, noticing the posters/brochures/ class schedule/ newspaper from the college. I noticed the student population was mostly Latino students. The school was in a predominately Latino community. After an hour or so, I made my way back to my car which was parked in the college parking lot.

As I walked to my car, I noticed the student from the hiring committee was walking toward the parking lot as well. She noticed me coming her way. She stopped walking to wait for me to catch up with her. I smiled and greeted her. We started talking. She told me she was a military veteran and a single mother. She said she returned to college so she could support her family. She told me even though she wasn't sure I was going to get a job offer, she wanted to know if I could be a mentor to her. She said she was really inspired by me, my life story, and the fact that I was interviewing for a leadership position at her school. She said she doesn't have any role models at her college, and she wanted to know if I was willing to talk to her about how to be successful in school. I said, "Of course!" so we exchanged contact information.

I did not get a job offer for that position. To this day I check on the job to see who got the offer. Nobody did. The job is still open, and the position keeps getting posted every few months. The institution obviously has a hard time establishing a solid candidate pool. I did not apply again for the position.

Even after all this time, what made this interview so unforgettable was that conversation I had with the student in the parking lot. That student made a major impact on me. She reminded me how important it is for me to be in a leadership position. She reminded me how important it is for our students to see people like me and her in leadership positions.

That student is my role model just as much as I am her role model. She has guts, determination, and focus. She is a true leader. She is the reason I do what I do!

With the need for culturally competent leaders so dire, it makes me wonder. Whatever happened to giving a person a chance? People CAN learn. In fact, there is abundant annual training provided through conferences and professional development for management. I understand sometimes candidates are not perfect matches for these positions, but everyone should be given a fair chance. After all, everyone has a learning curve when they take a new position. Especially when candidate pools run shallow, hiring managers should consider a person's potential for success just as much as previous experience.

I will never forget that interview. I will never forget our conversation in the college parking lot. She was a student looking anywhere and everywhere for a role model. I was in the right place at the right time. To this day it warms my heart to know I am on the right path. Even though I did not get the job offer, I got something better. I got a sense of purpose.

32

The Joy of Staying Busy When You Are Unemployed

For the long-term unemployed, days drag on endlessly. Day and night have no meaning. There is simply time spent lying in wait.

Mondays are the most exciting day of the week. Those are the days when you foolishly believe that something might come your way in terms of an interview or hiring decision. If you are registered with a temp agency (or six temp agencies, in my case), those are the days when assignments are usually offered. Yet, in my case, even that seems to rarely occur anymore. The lack of an offer to work on Monday means another week without a paycheck.

After 15 months of unemployment, you have run out of unemployment insurance, savings, pension, favors, sympathy, and patience.

In fact, after over a year of unemployment, you aren't even a statistic. You are off the radar. You are no longer eligible to make an unemployment claim, so you disappear from existence.

The long-term unemployed. That term sounds hopeless, and it has a matching stigma to boot. There are warnings about being unemployed this long. Articles discuss how people who are unemployed long-term are more likely to turn bitter, angry, thus we are harder to hire. Well, it is no wonder why. Any mature adult would be a little bitter after being out of work for over a year.

Yet, I still find it hard to believe that I have been unemployed for so long, let alone for 15 months! It is not as if I haven't tried looking for work. I have been on more than 50 interviews over the last year. I have even been a "finalist" about 50% of the time.

There have been numerous phone calls with hiring managers and college presidents telling me I interviewed fabulously, flawlessly, but that they are going with another candidate. These are never easy conversations. I have heard hiring managers attempt to explain their decision not to hire me in the nicest way possible. Some have displayed so much angst over the decision that I could hear their voices crack with emotion over the line. I have asked for feedback each time, with little or no real results.

Over 50 interviews and nothin' to show for it somehow feels ridiculous at this point. I have had up to 5 interviews in one week. I have had multiple days with 2 or more interviews in one day.

Even so, I cannot stop interviewing, I still need to find a job. I can't just stop looking. I can't rest without finding my next livelihood. I wish I could. Can I have a time out? Do I get a break?

So, after all these interviews, I feel I have acquired some wisdom that I can share about my job search. As a perpetual oversharer, allow me to indulge myself and to share with you some advice from an unsuccessful job search.

1. Always be nice and friendly

At the management level, the hiring committee regularly congratulates the candidate for being selected for an interview. While I might be on my 51st interview, the hiring committee does not know that. They are excited for you to be there. So as the candidate, your job is to be nice and friendly. You are making a first impression with the hiring committee as well as interviewing, so being nice and friendly will help you determine if the organization is a good fit for you. This interview is the first step in establishing a positive relationship with potential future colleagues.

2. Apply broadly

My background is in higher education administration, but mainly in the community college sector. Don't be afraid to apply across sectors, such as research four-year and private universities, state, and proprietary institutions as well as other public and private sector organizations. I have interviewed at many different levels for different types of organizations. I have applied for work in government, health care, education, general customer service, management, for-profit as well as non-profit. You will get an interview if you have the skills, knowledge, and experience that transfers across sectors. Hiring managers do interview candidates across different sectors.

3. Apply multiple times

I have applied for multiple positions at the same organization. I have even been a final candidate multiple times for different positions at the same organization. Each position has a different hiring committee. If your skills and experience match the open position, then you have an equal chance. Hiring managers want someone interested in their organization. If you have that interest, then let it show.

4. The long-term unemployed are un-hirable

I would like to think that being unemployed does not automatically disqualify one from getting a job. I have received many invitations to interview, so being unemployed certainly does not disqualify one from being interviewed. But what about receiving a job offer? Unfortunately, I have heard straight from the horse's mouth that one DOES need a job to get a job. I was told by a very near and dear mentor that they would never hire someone who doesn't already have a job. The exact quote was, "I would never hire someone who is currently unemployed". This person is a chancellor responsible for hiring 100's in a four-college district. So, there's that…

5. "Open" positions

Not all "open" positions are truly open. Some job searches are called off by the organization, even after final interviews have taken place. I have been on "final" interviews and had references checked only to be told that the organization decided not to fill the position. There are several reasons why the positions are not filled. Sometimes the position is re-classified, changed from a temporary/interim position to a permanent position or the job responsibilities are added/removed so the organization decided to re-open the position later. Sometimes the candidate pool for the first recruitment is used to identify the talent pipeline in an organization. Internal candidates are given the opportunity to experience the interview process so they can identify potential gaps in their professional development. This is a method to encourage potential future leaders at the organization. There are other reasons that a position might go unfilled, but open positions do not mean that the organization is going to hire for those positions.

6. Internal candidate advantage

Depending on the organization, internal candidates can have an advantage over external candidates. It is true that internal candidates would be better familiarized with processes, personnel, issues, solutions, and initiatives for specific organizations. I have seen many positions filled with internal candidates that obviously bring intimate knowledge to the position that would be hard to compete against as an outsider. In addition, there is the "halo effect" where people prefer to hire like-minded candidates. Who is better like-minded than someone who has worked at the organization day after day? If the organization is a healthy, positive place, then the internal candidate certainly has the advantage because presumably people enjoy working together and want to see each other be successful. If the organization is unhealthy and toxic, then the opposite might be true and the internal candidate might be at a disadvantage, but who wants to work there?

7. Be your best, truest self

Interview after interview, one begins to wonder if his/her personality is the problem. After all, skills, knowledge, experience are a concrete, unchangeable attribute, but personality is malleable and can present itself in different ways depending on the environment. With that in mind, I have had the opportunity to test out this theory a few times. I have gone on some interviews as a shy, quiet, introvert, wallflower and on other interviews as an extrovert, outgoing, social butterfly. I have made hiring committee members laugh, cry, smile, and cheer over stories I have told in interviews. I have attempted to come across as introspective and contemplative and then as debonair and charismatic. In the end, the result was the same. What matters most is to be authentic, open, honest, and true to your strengths. In the end, my sense of personal integrity is what matters the most to my role as a leader, so the personality I bring will only add value to a leadership team.

8. Hiring committee friends

There will be interviews where you know someone on the hiring committee. You might even know a few people or the entire committee. If you have 15 years of experience like me, you are bound to have professional contacts at many different institutions. I have been on interviews where the entire committee was made up of former colleagues and close, personal friends. Even with friends on the hiring committee, there are no guarantees that you will receive a job offer. You could have close friends, former colleagues, and real buddies on the committee, but that doesn't mean you are their first choice. Always be professional and do your best to show you are the best candidate. It is always a competition, and it is up to you to make your application stand out.

9. Being overqualified

Your job in the interview is to get the job offer. You need to have ready answers for all kinds of questions. I am someone who has worked in higher education of over 15 years. How can I get a job in sales, or customer sales, or government when all my experience is so one-dimensional and at such a high level? I have been told by hiring managers that they are worried I would get "bored" or "run out of things to do" in a position. Honestly, there was one time when I was on an interview and excused myself halfway through because I was overqualified and not interested in that particular job. But I still need a job. So now, I directly address being overqualified and my awareness that I am intentionally taking a demotion or applying for low-level positions to gain new experience. I sell my clear love of learning and my passion for taking on challenging roles.

10. Stay positive

I have had well-meaning friends tell me it is time to brush ego aside and to beg, plead, guilt my way to a job offer. I have been encouraged to play the "race" or diversity card, talk about being a single mother, tell managers I am on state cash aid and food stamps. Some people have recommended I apologize and take the blame for being unemployed for so long. As a person who has been a hiring manager in the past, I cannot imagine any scenario where a candidate begging for a job would result in an offer to hire. Instead, I feel that I need to stay positive, be optimistic, have hope for the future, and continue to believe that my skills, knowledge, and experience are valuable as is. People want to hire positive people, not someone who is desperate and emotional.

So, I have learned some valuable lessons in my state of unemployment. I hope these tips are helpful to others who are long-term unemployed like me.

Even so, I have racked my brain coming up with ways to

occupy my time between these never-ending interviews. I have found some positive ways to stay busy. In my downtime I have tried out a few new ideas:

Opened my own consulting firm (I am now president/owner of Elan Vital Research Group)

Created online content on a variety of professional development topics (LinkedIn)

Decided to gain new knowledge and a new career pathway (beginning a 2nd Master of Arts Degree, in teaching)

Launched an online informational channel (YouTube, "Lily College Mythbusters")

Joined local and national organizations (California Hispanic Chamber of Commerce)

Achieved fitness goals and on-going healthy habits (hiked 16-mile trail)

Maintained professional contacts and mentees

Researched additional certifications and professional development

While this time off work can feel interminable and my efforts to find a job can feel futile, I remain hopeful. The hiring process is complex and mysterious. All I can do is keep changing the channel to see if anything else is on.

I do know one thing for sure, I can't wait for a job to live my life. Life goes on.

33

Being Excellent While Unemployed

Every day is an opportunity to do something extraordinary. Now, doing something extraordinary does not always mean making a huge, significant change. It can mean any number of small, random acts of kindness. The point is to do something positive and to stop putting it off!

Each day there are literally dozens of opportunities to do something extraordinary. Each time you decide, there is an opportunity to change the world in a positive way, be it big or small. The trick is to be mindful of these opportunities as they present themselves and to ask yourself, "Am I making a decision based on fear or based on doing something extraordinary?"

What is it about mediocrity that makes it so tempting to allow it to continue uninterrupted? Unfortunately, mediocrity is often what feels most comfortable, simplest, familiar, safest, and/or neatest compared to raising the standard. In many instances, it is simply easiest to maintain the status quo. For many people, the desire for self-preservation often trumps the desire for self-exploration and discovery.

The importance of maintaining our sense of equilibrium or homeostasis cannot be denied. And while there is comfort in having balance in our life, it is equally as important for leaders to possess a drive to break the cycle of mediocrity that often plagues our daily lives.

As a leader, it is our duty to disrupt mediocrity, to break cycles of preservation over exploration and discovery. For it is in the disruption that the extraordinary can happen. Therefore, it is of the utmost importance that space is allotted for the extraordinary to exist.

The question we must ask ourselves as leaders is, "Am I being a disruptor of mediocrity?"

Or as Bill S. Preston, Esq. suggested in the movie Bill and Ted's Excellent Adventure (1989), ask yourself "Am I being excellent?"

34

Patience is a Bear

A watched pot never boils

Patience is a virtue…

Patience by Guns n Roses… sing it, Axl!

In this day and age of instant gratification, waiting to hear back about a hiring decision can feel like a form of slow torture. Especially when you have been out of the job market for an extended amount of time, the wait for a decision about a potential job offer can be both exhilarating and terrifying. What if you get the job offer? Hurray! What about if you don't? Down the deep pit of despair!

I have been out of work for one year now. It feels like forever. Since that time, I have been through quite the personal journey/struggle of understanding my future prospects and potential in the current job market.

What do you do if you have painted yourself into a metaphorical corner of a professional industry? Do you give up and start from scratch, or stay the course and start climbing the walls? You start to wonder if you have the skills to get out and try something else. Whatever you do decide to do, you need to have patience for yourself and your situation.

I have never been one to tout patience as a personal strength of mine. In fact, I am the opposite, a fast learner, driven, ambitious, focused, energetic, strategic, future minded, and determined. I have never used patient to describe myself until recently. But I must face the facts that the reality is I don't have a choice in the matter. I must be patient and I am learning the value of slowing things down.

Time keeps on ticking.

I used to feel anxious about my long-term goals, even my own sense of mortality. After all, my mother passed away at the age of 37. I used to have this irrational fear and transfer it into a sense of urgency about my career. I felt I needed to accomplish as much as possible before I turned the dreaded age of 37. As if that age was some sort of self-fulfilling prophecy or omen to my own untimely demise. This fear is a common enough sentiment. I have met other people with parents who died early; I hear again and again how they feared turning the age when their own parents passed on. Even still, I applied that fear to my work and my life goals.

Interestingly, I created a career path that came together through happenstance and serendipity. Early in life I found a passion and a means of personal fulfillment through my career. I found a way of intertwining my sense of self in a career that had a clear roadmap to success. I found my life's work in serving a unique and specific niche in the industry of higher education by the time I was 20 years old. I knew then that I wanted to be a community college president one day. Lucky for me, all I needed to do was execute my plan.

Best laid plans of mice and men often go awry.

So, life happened. I was going full steam ahead. I got my education. Check. I had a family. Check. I got promoted. Check. I reached a certain salary milestone. Check. I re-located to a geographic location I always dream of. Check. I even turned 37 years old without dying, yippee! Check. Then last summer 2014, I got laid off, lost my house, used up my entire retirement/life savings, maxed out all my credit cards, got on welfare/food stamps, the whole nine yards - now what?

Do I throw in the towel and give up? No way. Nope.

Life is a marathon, not a sprint.

Chapter 34

While I have had no luck so far in finding a job in my field, nothing is preventing me from taking a step back. Perhaps I take a job just to make ends meet for a while. Perhaps I slow things down and stop to smell the roses for once.

I know where my passion is, but I still need to put bread on the table. I have learned to have patience. For 13 years, I was lucky to have a career that meant so much to me, but now I need to think about my family first. So maybe I don't go back to doing exactly what I was doing before, or maybe a new opportunity will present itself. Either way I have learned to think of the long game not just what I think I should be doing instead. I need to re-prioritize because try as I might to control the universe, I have no influence over whether or not I get that job offer. I will get there eventually without a doubt. But for now, I need to have a little patience.

35

When the Star Player is Benched

I am a team player. I am accommodating, conscientious, respectful, communicative, considerate, and focused on shared goals. I inherently consider the collective good over my own personal needs when making decisions as a leader.

I often wonder if my sense of shared responsibility as a leader is due to my being raised in a single parent household with four siblings and very limited resources. My siblings and I certainly had to be creative starting out in life with so little support.

When I was growing up, there was never enough money, food, clothes, heating/hot water, bathroom time, space to sleep, school supplies, and certainly no privacy. With very little to claim as my own, my family was what mattered the most.

The family unit was paramount, and we were all equal members of the team. So, when decisions within the family had to be made, we regularly had thorough discussions about whose turn it was to do what and why. We kids learned to be astute negotiators, advocating for our fair share. Yet, more times than not we felt jilted and shortchanged since we never fully got our way. We always had to share, compromise, or take turns.

Faced with extreme scarcity of resources, I understood that the basic principle within my family for making decisions was this notion of fairness and equal participation. To think about the good of the team. My upbringing gave me a foundation for my basic beliefs about democracy and decision making.

During job interviews, I am often asked about my leadership style and how I make decisions. My years of professional experience managing people, projects, budgets, grants, and special programs provides me with ample material to draw from to describe my leadership qualities. Yet, it is also my upbringing and my family that has shaped who I am as a leader.

The way I describe my leadership style is that I see myself being a coach for a team. Looking at the strengths of the people and the resources of the organization, I make decisions to be fair, inclusive, and decisive.

I am currently on the sidelines of my career being unemployed for the last eight months. In a way I feel like I got benched by the coach. But still, I wait patiently for my turn to get back in the game. I know my time will come.

Even so, I will never forget my humble beginnings. I will always use those experiences as a lesson in how to be fair and resourceful in my professional life. As well, I will always remember to be a mentor to others, as there are other players who deserve a chance to play for the team too!

36

The F Word - Feedback

Feedback. Constructive criticism. Positive reinforcement. Negative reinforcement. Evaluation. Performance review. These are words that often elicit the fight or flight response. It can be just as uncomfortable for the person to give feedback as it can be for the person to receive it. Yet, during a job search you are constantly under review but there is no easy way to receive feedback other than receiving a job offer. What a situation!

As leaders, one of the badges of honor is one's ability to handle feedback. One must be adept at both doling it out and in receiving it. One must be tactful, discreet, honest, direct, respectful, and humble in times when conversations involve discussing one's job performance. There is a clear delineation between the role of the manager and the employee in providing feedback. It is a top-down process. When there is the 360-performance review, then it is an inclusive and comprehensive process. As well, there are many informal and non-structured ways to provide feedback, depending on the relationships between staff and management. Within the structure of an organization there is ample opportunity to give and receive feedback.

What about receiving feedback during a job search? As an interviewee you try to interpret your performance at the interview by people's verbal reactions, body language, and of course whether or not you are invited back for an additional interview. Ultimately, the final seal of approval is the official job offer.

But other than receiving a job offer, there is no other feedback offered to the candidate. I have been on the hiring manager side many times in my career. I have seen people bomb interviews. I have seen people blow interviews because of their appearance, use of inappropriate anecdotes, nerves, and other issues that came up that detracted from their skills and experience that got them the interview in the first place. Oftentimes I had lamented that there is no suitable mechanism to alert the candidate about how to improve their interview skills. As well, there have been candidates that ace the interview, but the position was given to a different candidate for various reasons.

As someone currently on the job search, I am again intimately aware of how closed off the candidate feels during the interview process. I have been out of work for almost six months. In that time, I have been on dozens of interviews. I have been a "finalist" nine times. That means over the last six months, I have been advanced nine times to the final round of interviews, yet not one job offer. Close, but no cigar.

While I prep and organize myself for each interview with the utmost care, one thing I feel is missing in this whole process is a way to receive feedback. It would be invaluable for me to be able to have a short conversation about what I could do to improve my chances for next time.

Therefore, the feedback I would like to provide to hiring managers is to encourage them to take a little time with final candidates to provide meaningful feedback to them so they can improve for the next interview. When I was a hiring manager, I certainly tried to provide some feedback to the final candidates, and I will continue to do so in the future. I understand it can be a very awkward conversation, but it is through these difficult conversations that people learn and develop their skills. Feedback should not be a dirty word; it should be a way to get a conversation going in a positive direction.

37

The Power of the Forces of Good and Evil

Friends versus enemies. Good versus evil. Allies versus detractors. The rebellion versus the Dark Side. Everywhere you go there are forces of good and evil. Your success as a leader depends on your ability to triumph over evil. How you develop your professional network and how you build support within your organization to move your ideas forward often depends on how you develop your community of allies.

As a leader, one of the most important skills to have is the ability to build your community of allies. After all, how can you call yourself a leader if you have no followers?

I had a great lesson in the importance of building a community of allies after working in an extremely toxic work environment. It was seven years ago, and I was assigned to work in a volatile department that was known to have several bad apples, poor performance outcomes, regular employee and customer complaints, flagrant misuse of resources, and absolutely no leadership from the previous managers who perceived the department to be a stepping stone to bigger and better positions. I accepted the short-term assignment as manager with the hopes of developing my knowledge and skills to be able to accept the permanent assignment when it became available.

Within a few weeks, after meeting with upper management about goals, strategy, performance standards, and expectations, I began to implement major changes to clean up the various messes of the department. It was always in my heart to improve the department for the betterment of the organization. I had some wonderful ideas and the full support of my supervisors and executives in the organization who knew my background and abilities. What I did not have was the support of the "troops on the ground" so to speak, the staff and community who were on the receiving end of all the improvements I was attempting to implement.

The first hints of trouble began when I attended a large-scale event on campus where I lamented with a staff member in a different department, on how I wished my own department had greater visibility at the event. In fact, there was no representation of my own department at the event. By the time I made my way back to my department, word had spread across the organization that I had put my staff down in public, taking what I had said out of context.

From there it seemed as if every word I said was scrutinized and met with skepticism and doubt. During staff meetings there were complaints about my plans and goals that had already received prior approval from upper management. Day by day I faced resistance and outright refusal to put into place departmental actions necessary to implement the turnaround of the department.

Then one day I was informed that there was a petition delivered to management demanding no less than my resignation from that department. The issues that were brought forward included my strict adherence to department budgeting practices, public statements taken out of context, and my being out of touch with the mission of the department. It was a hard pill to swallow to see that my actions were being misinterpreted and misunderstood. After all, I had only the best of intentions when I began the assignment. In fact, management was thrilled with the progress I had made in my short tenure, but I had no support from my staff and the community.

Not only did I have no support within my department, but now it seemed that there was an outright conspiracy to sabotage all the progress being made. There were lies, innuendos, backstabbing, accusations, and complete distrust between myself and my staff. Any attempt I made to remedy the situation only seemed to make matters worse. In the end, I fulfilled the obligations of the assignment and decided to move on from the organization at the end of the term.

I could have decided to fight for my position and to take a stand. I knew what I was doing was for the betterment of the department. I had support from management and colleagues within the organization who encouraged me to hold fast. After a year at the organization, I had a small community of allies who said I was the best thing to ever happen to that department. The CEO even told me I managed to make more improvements in one year than the handful of managers who came before me. There were staff in other departments who encouraged me to transfer to their department. It seemed as if everyone wanted me to stay except the people in my own department.

I decided to leave the organization due to the fact that I was offered a new position in my hometown. It was at an organization that I knew, and people knew me. It was a position where I was welcomed with open arms.

One of the first things I did in my new position was to get to know my staff. I let them get to know me, who I was, and where I came from. I discussed the years of my experience and my knowledge in the field. I explained my hopes and dreams for the department and inquired about the hopes the staff had for the department. As well, I got to know other managers and staff in the organization. I invited people to lunch and accepted invitations to other department events. I put myself out there to be seen and to see how other departments run their business.

Quickly I received support from my new colleagues and staff. I was elected to chair meetings and appointed to high-level committees. I was encouraged to develop new programs and plans for the department. It was night and day compared to my previous assignment.

I knew I had won the support of the organization the day the CEO walked into my office to inform me that he had just nominated me to participate in a two-year leadership development program for future CEO's. It was both an honor and a privilege, but I did not forget to be humbled by reality, how it took a great deal of hard work to lead up to that moment.

The lessons I learned have shaped my work as a leader. I realized that whenever I accept a position of leadership, I am faced with new people and new situations that test my strength of character. The friends and allies that I chose to make at my organization can lead to my triumph or my downfall. Only by having a community of allies can I develop myself, my legacy, and my organization. One way my success as a leader can be measured is by my community of allies. And I say, the more the merrier!

38

Taking a Career Pause

Most days I keep busy with my little routine. There is always something that needs to get done. I apply for work each day. Without fail.

Of course, I used to have a very different schedule. I used to rush, check my wristwatch, zip by, and sail through the day. Now the days have a slower pace.

While there is always a chore or an errand, most days it is never anything that cannot be put off to the next day.

I used to hold meetings with the president or with hiring committees or department members. These days the only must-do items on my daily calendar consist of walking my dog and shuttling my young son to school.

Sometimes I think about my working-self compared to my unemployed self. A song comes to mind, Somebody That I Used to Know, http://www.azlyrics.com/lyrics/gotye/somebodythatiusedtoknow.html. I used to know myself as a busy, rushed, preoccupied, hasty, never enough time to do anything person.

Now I am a person without a schedule, all the time in the world, staring at the clock on the wall waiting for the hours to slowly pass me by with little to show for another day of my life.

Being out of work for any extended amount of time affords plenty of opportunity for reflection. I think about what I *want* to do or *might* do, rather than what do I *have* to do. I no longer have the luxury to think about what I *get* to do.

With all the time in the world to plan new days, I am amazed with how so little gets done. When I was busy and working, I always felt that I was doing so much. Even when I felt like I never had enough time.

These days, I have entered a state of inertia. The law of inertia states that: A body will preserve its velocity and direction so long as no force in its motion's direction acts on it. With no outside force acting on my time, I am preserving a state of inactivity.

In reflecting on my state of inactivity, I have learned a great deal about myself. What I have developed is a better sense of who I am and what I am looking for in my next position. In addition, I have a better grasp of the type of person I want to be for my family and friends.

It is a luxury to have time to pause and think about your life and its trajectory. Do I want to learn to cook, learn a new language, get in top physical fitness, learn to crotchet, what? For me, the answer is I want to take time to do nothing.

Why not take a break? I have accomplished a great deal for my age and my position in life. I have done more in my life up to this point than I ever thought possible. I have travelled to wonderful countries like China, Cuba, and Canada (yes, all C countries for some reason). I have driven solo from San Francisco to Boston, lived on the east and west coast. I have completed my education to the terminal level for my field with my doctorate degree. I have published academic research. I have advanced far in my field and will likely continue to advance. I am raising my young son in a fun and loving environment. I have enjoyed good health and competed in 10k's and fun runs. I have attended professional conferences and life/work balance workshops.

So maybe it is the right time to do nothing while I can enjoy it. The time will come when I am dashing off, checking my wristwatch, and sailing through the day again. For now, I will be a couch potato.

39

Loving Thoughts on Being a College Intern

I loved being a college intern! I was in a graduate program in New York City that required a year-long internship as part of my master's degree in Student Personnel Administration which was within the higher education administration department. I was fortunate enough to gain an internship working at a medical school in the Office of Minority Affairs helping with a college preparation program for students of color interested in science, technology, engineering, and math (STEM). It was the perfect environment to learn how to apply the student development theories I was learning about with the practical experience of the reality of working on a college campus.

It was there that I gained experience in advising students about career and college preparation, evaluating learning outcomes of a college enrichment program, writing, and reporting on a federal grant, conducting classroom observations, hiring, and training preceptors on curriculum development and teaching methods, leading monthly staff meetings, developing and assessing student development workshops, and so much more.

It was exactly the experience I needed to launch my career in student services. Even now, 12 years later, I use some of the skills I gained during my internship in my role as a college administrator.

Plus, I know for a fact that I never would have landed my first job in student services if it wasn't for my internship experience. Having direct experience working with students and student services program management is often a minimum requirement for most entry-level positions at a community college.

Working in student services requires a person to have professional competencies in a myriad of areas. Professionals in this area are required to be competent in working with various offices on the college campus to student advising to program evaluation to employee relations to knowing state and federal education policy to strategic planning and assessment to proficiencies in working with a diverse student population. So how do you develop these competencies if you have never worked on a college campus?

The value of internships is without question. There are abundant studies and pathways for internships for students and faculty that underscore their value. A quick internet search produces several wonderful opportunities for students and faculty in community college to gain experience.

Most community college campuses have a Career Center where internship opportunities are advertised or Cooperative Education or Work Experience programs where assistance is provided to help students locate opportunities and earn college credit for related work experience. Then there are campus-sponsored faculty internship programs geared towards developing experience in the community college setting.

Below are a few programs geared towards these purposes:

For community college student internships,
http://science.energy.gov/wdts/cci/
http://foundationccc.org/WhatWeDo/StudentJobs/tabid/356/Default.aspx
http://www.pasadena.edu/studentservices/careercenter/internship.cfm
http://www.nasa.gov/centers/ames/education/internships/#.VEfZTSgm17F

For California community college faculty internships,
http://www.laccd.edu/Employment/Pages/Project-

MATCH.aspx,
   http://interwork.sdsu.edu/main/sdiccca/
   http://www.cccregistry.org/jobs/miscelaneous/resources.aspx#Heading12
   http://agency.governmentjobs.com/lbcc/default.cfm?action=viewjob&JobID=298397&headerfooter=1&WDDXJobSearchParams=
   http://web.peralta.edu/facultydiversity/
   https://www.ccsf.edu/en/about-city-college/administration/chancellors-office/diversity_internships.html

Internships are the key to developing professional skills and the leadership pipeline in the community college sector. So what are the opportunities for potential professionals interested in student services in the community college sector?

Unfortunately, there are not many formal internship programs for student services personnel that I am aware. I have worked at six different community colleges. Each one has different board policy when it comes to internship/unpaid/volunteer opportunities for staff due to the complex and unique nature of collective bargaining (union) agreements and local practices within specific college districts.

The opportunity to intern can vary greatly from campus to campus. I have worked at college campuses where there are abundant opportunities for internships with wonderful, established partnerships with the local universities to campuses where college leadership was unaware or highly suspicious and resistant to the very idea of interns citing Fair Labor Standards Act, http://www.dol.gov/whd/regs/compliance/whdfs71.htm, with no support or process to provide internship opportunity for staff and/or management.

Since internships are a value to the organization and the professional development of future employees, I believe it is our duty to provide these opportunities in the community college sector. For this reason, I encourage our leaders at college campuses to support and develop internship opportunities for students, faculty, and student services staff alike. It is a fantastic way to give back to the community and to develop meaningful partnerships with our university colleagues.

40

HRMS Blues

I have established a certain routine to my job search. Whenever I see a job posted that looks even remotely interesting, I prepare to customize my cover letter detailing my qualifications based on the job description and my 12 years of experience. I gather ready-made PDF documents like my resume, personal references, salary history, and letters of reference, unofficial college transcripts, and statements on my philosophy of leadership and diversity.

Then comes the time when I need to complete the job application or create a profile in the human resource management system (HRMS) of the organization. Here is where the exciting part comes...

I have been on the job search for the last year looking for a job in the public sector. I have become familiar with various employee application software programs as a result. Many places that I am applying to use similar systems such as Neogov, Vitae, or another similar HRMS system. My confidence in using these systems has grown as I have applied to dozens of positions. I am confident in my resume, cover letter, and other supporting documents. I have landed over 15 interviews in the last four months. While I continue to interview in the hopes of receiving a job offer, I continue to apply for open positions.

What I have noticed is that there is a huge amount of variety in the ways employment applications are processed from organization to organization. In the last six months, I have experienced applying for a job using a paper application that must be sent via snail mail to using employee application software that imports all pertinent data from an uploaded resume.

In many instances there is a unique employment application that must be completed for each open position, in addition to the standard ready-made documents such as resume, cover letter, personal references, etc.

Some organizations are using a shared HRMS database that allows me to use the same profile to apply to multiple positions at different campuses. That is a good way to save the candidate some valuable time and a headache or two for sure!

When a job opens for an organization where I have a profile already in the HRMS database, I can apply and attach all my uniquely tailored materials in as little as 15 minutes! Yeah!

If I need to create a new profile in a new HRMS program, I know there is a slight chance that I might not be able to apply for the position at all. Why is that you might ask?

I consider myself an intelligent person. I have applied for 100's of jobs over my career. I attended college, earned my Associate of Arts degree, Bachelor of Arts degree, Master of Arts degree, and have earned a doctorate. Yet, there are currently some HRMS programs that I simply do not have the patience for or technical assistance to help with the glitches!

I believe when you are out of work, you need to apply for everything and anything that means a steady paycheck and a match between your interests and abilities. Yet, there are some HRMS fails that have prevented me from submitting my application simply because I could not figure out how to search/abbreviate my state or the name of the country where I went to college!

I was on one organization's website for over one hour creating a profile meticulously going from screen to screen. I was hitting the "Save and Continue" button at the bottom of each screen. I got to the next to last screen and I inadvertently land on a different screen completely outside the HRMS pages. In the past I have been able to log back in and retrieve the saved work.

Chapter 40

In this particular instance, when I logged back in, nothing was saved. Nothing was saved…

Do I begin all over again from scratch? Do I scream into a pillow? Do I re-think applying to the organization? Do I sometimes give up? Yes, yes, yes, and yes! C'mon, man!

When I am applying for a job, I am often comparing the organization with other organizations and comparing one HRMS with another HRMS. Some HRMS programs I can whiz through without a second thought. Even the paper application process does not throw me off. I can print out the paper application and mail it off with my other application materials with the good ol' USPS, easy, peasy!

But when I am faced with an HRMS program that takes me all day to create a unique and extraordinary password with exotic characters and password hints, complete my home address or employment history or educational history in addition to attaching the requisite resume, cover letter, references, unofficial transcripts, and other supplemental materials, I often move on to the next organization.

Over the last ten months, I have applied to almost 100 different positions. I expect to continue to be applying for positions until I receive a confirmed job offer.

While I am currently unemployed and extremely eager to land a new position, the reality is that I do not HAVE to apply for every job I see. My personal belief that I should apply for every job I see fails to consider that some HRMS programs make it easier said than done.

So, in the future, I will pay considerable attention to the HRMS at my future employers with new eyes. Hiring and recruiting new employees is critical to building the human capacity of any organization. Unfortunately, right now, I am learning more lessons on what NOT to do in the hiring process based off all these miserable HRMS program fails.

Still, as I work through this period of my unemployment,

I am learning lessons about the hiring process that will be an asset to my career in administration. I am starting to feel like an expert on various HRMS programs and that provides me with a great experience for the future!

41

Diversity, Equity, and Inclusion for the New Generation

It is exciting to see a new generation of young celebrities tackle the issues of diversity that constantly plague our great country. In the last couple of weeks, I have heard many opinions from young adults voicing concern about diversity issues. There was Emma Watson, Taylor Swift, and others tackling feminism, Candace Cameron tackling female sexuality. Then came Raven-Symone tackling queer and racial identity.

As a student affairs professional working with college students, I am very aware that our identity is important to our personal development. I have studied gender identity development, racial identity development, cognitive development, and social-emotional development theories. Research shows that young adults from 18-25 years of age develop their sense of identity and sense of who they are in relation to the world around them. Ideally, attending college and developing your sense of identity is one way to develop a sense of who you are and a way to identify your personal beliefs.

What I find interesting about these young celebrities expressing opinions about feminism, homophobia, and other diversity issues is that they are often using their celebrity with good intentions, but they fail to consider the developmental aspect of identity development.

Often young adults are quick to dismiss labels that feel uncomfortable or awkward. Racism, sexism, homophobia, discrimination, harassment, classism, agesim, ableism, and such are labels that are politically loaded terms. It takes careful research and studying to really learn where these labels came from and why they matter in our society. Diversity issues are sticky, tricky, and ongoing.

Some people prefer to see our society as a post-racial or post-sexist society. The democratic ideals that our country was founded is an ongoing work in progress.

When I hear Emma Watson addressing the United Nations on the topic of feminism or Raven-Symone telling Oprah Winfrey that she is not an African American, the younger generation is searching for a new meaning of what it means to be and their sense of identity. I have faith in the generation coming of age in these trying times, but there is a need to provide historical context and interconnections to how these concepts are interrelated across groups.

In Racial Identity Development models there are several stages that people go through to develop their sense of identity. Some of the stages are as follows:

Conformity -> Dissonance -> Resistance and Immersion -> Introspection -> Synergistic Articulation and Awareness

People move through these stages at varying degrees and for different reasons. There are external and internal factors that can move a person along their development.

More information about racial identity theories can be found at:

http://studentdevelopmenttheory.wordpress.com/racial-identity-development/

These young adults are going through a journey of their identity and there should be room for their development to happen. Unfortunately, these stars are developing their identity in the limelight of the media with little room for forgiveness.

We know that diversity issues are constantly under discussion. One only need to look at current events to see headlines about Ferguson, MO, or the Ebola outbreak in Africa, or the sexual assaults on college campuses, or domestic violence in the

Chapter 41

NFL and other arenas, fascination about Bruce Jenner's gender transition, the White House intruder, etc. These headlines grab our attention because they highlight undercurrents about diversity issues that we face as a society.

When I worked as the Director of a campus cultural center, I used my position to provide a platform for understanding diversity issues at the college. There would be panel discussions and guest speakers invited to address topics that affect our identity. People often consider diversity issues as fluff, but they are real and affect our personal development as college students and as employees. Management must provide venues for these conversations to happen and to support our students and employees.

What I have noticed is that young adults want to redefine the terms or shun labels altogether. While labels can be empowering, they can be a burden as well. The terms and labels may change but the work to create inclusion, opportunity, and equity in our society remains the same.

It is exciting to see new attention on issues of discrimination, bias, injustice, and harassment. I am hopeful that the world is seeing that labels do not fix problems and vocabulary terms do not provide solutions.

What is needed is people working together, people committed to making a difference. I see people willing to step up and speak their mind without allowing a label to limit their purpose. The synergy from working across social divisions will be the only way that we can work toward finding solutions to our society's problems. I applaud young adults working toward constructing a brave new world on their terms where there is inclusion, respect, and representation. Hopefully, they will get the support they need as they find their way.

42

Career Advancement in Student Services in Higher Education

The year was 2002. I had just got my first full-time position working in student services at a community college. It was my dream job! I thought I would stay in that position forever.

A month into my new job I heard rumblings about staff layoffs and statewide budget cuts. Then I heard about the hiring freeze at the college. Next, there were discussions about staff longevity rankings. After that came conversations about "bumping rights". Eventually, union stewards were calling meetings with staff and the ugly reality of layoffs was hitting the college hard.

I was a complete newbie to the world of collective bargaining agreements (CBA's), but I was selected to sit on a college staff negotiations committee to discuss the employee bargaining position. At the same time, I was eager to be a part of the college workings and found myself aiding in the accreditation process as well as developing my role in student services.

Even so, after four months in my dream job, I received a layoff notice. Another employee was using their bumping rights to take my position. All of a sudden I realized I needed to start looking for work. But where to start?

Whether you are looking to change positions out of necessity or to advance your career, learning about career advancement in student services is important if we are to develop future leaders in the community college sector.

As I have mentioned in previous posts, there is heavy

competition in obtaining a position in student services at a California community college. How do you make your application stand out and how do you advance your career once you obtain one of these coveted positions?

Timing is Everything

How long should you stay in a position before you decide to move on? When I was laid off, I had less than a year of community college work experience. Yet during that time I had made significant contributions to the school. I had developed a new online newsletter, led a campus-wide initiative, increased visibility of the department and the website, and participated in campus committees such as accreditation and CBA negotiations. Then I was forced to leave due to the layoff. I had no choice. I needed a new job.

Over my career, I have been in positions for as little as 8 months to just shy of four years. I have learned that the length of time you have held a position is not as important as the contributions you have made during your time in each position. For someone new to the field, it is best to have a solid year under your belt before you consider a new position. Your application will move to the top of the pile if you can show that you have made important contributions in each position you have held.

Understand Lateral Transfers

Student service staff positions at California community colleges are union jobs. Most school districts are under a CBA that provides for lateral transfers within the same district. Depending on the specific language of your district, you can apply for a lateral transfer within your district to move from one position to another in a different department. This means if you are a Specialist in the Outreach Department and a Specialist position opens in the Career Center, you can be considered as a lateral transfer, helping you gain an interview! Having experience in different offices will help your application stand out when you apply for that promotion.

Once you have experienced different departments, you can determine where you want to advance in your career to the management level. Experience across departments will help you decide if a management career is worth pursuing.

Know Staff Hierarchy

Having a sense of the college staffing structure and your place in it can help you understand your career better. Every college categorizes their positions in a unique manner. Depending on the size of the college and the departments there can be positions such as Career Generalist or Assistant Director of EOPS or Associate Vice President or combined positions. Generally, a career in student services can have a trajectory that goes something like this:

Staff Assistant -> Generalist -> Specialist -> Coordinator -> Director/Manager -> Dean -> Vice President -> President

If someone begins in student services as a counselor then they are a faculty member and will have a trajectory that goes something like this:

Faculty Member -> Dean -> Vice President -> President

When you are applying for a new position in student services, you should look to advance your position to the next level to develop new skills. If you are currently a staff assistant and you are applying for another staff assistant position, there might be questions about why you are not applying for a higher-level position.

Leaving/Changing Schools and/or Districts

With 116 colleges across the state of California, you should consider different schools if you are looking for career advancement. It is rare for someone to remain at the same school their entire career, unless they remain in the same position. In addition, many times a person becomes so entrenched in a particular role, it can be hard to break free from that for career advancement. Working at different schools provides a deeper understanding of the community college system and helps your application when it comes time to apply for a promotion.

Furthering Your Education

Working in the field of higher education means that your educational history matters. There are many positions where a certain degree is required such as Counseling or Disability Services. Some positions require very little education perhaps an associate of art degree. To advance in your career, you will need to decide if you want to further your education. It is a big decision that affects your life and your future. It is critical to look at your career to see if your education will match the goals you have in mind.

Having the wrong degree can hinder your plans. For example, someone with a master's degree in higher education administration might want to pursue a career as a college counselor. In this scenario it will be an extremely difficult road to trudge to be a counselor because most job announcements require a master's degree in counseling. While there is the opportunity to gain equivalency, it is an uphill battle. While that kind of degree might work at other institutions of higher education such as state universities and private and proprietary schools, the state community college system is very specific in the hiring requirements for faculty, see Minimum Faculty Hiring Qualifications for more information, http://extranet.cccco.edu/Portals/1/AA/MinQuals/MinimumQualificationsHandbook2012_2014.pdf.

Having that advanced degree gives your application the edge you need to advance in your career.

Accept Interim/Substitute/Backfill Assignments

Taking a position on an interim basis is a good way to learn more about a position or department. As well, you gain an opportunity to test your skills and knowledge before you commit to a permanent position. These assignments are often for a predetermined amount of time, usually for less than a year or as much as one or more years while the college looks for a permanent replacement.

Make sure you determine if you are eligible to apply for the permanent position before you accept the position. Always remember that taking an interim assignment is no guarantee that you will be selected for the permanent position, so have a backup plan.

It is helpful to note that interim (but not substitute or backfill) assignments are generally given the same weight as a permanent position in the applicant review process. As well, these temporary positions can help you gain skills you might not otherwise have access to such as supervisory experience.

Apply for the Safe and the Just Out of Reach

It takes persistence and determination to advance in your career. Your career may have a series of detours, nosedives, stalls, and sidetracks before it gains momentum. Or you might luck out and get every job you ever apply to on the first try. I have seen both scenarios play out. I know someone who only applied for three jobs their entire career after graduate school, they went from faculty then promoted to dean (at the same school) to vice president to president. Then I know someone who has been applying for a promotion going on over five years now with no results. My advice is to apply for everything that you see fit. It is your life!

Your career is your choice. Only you can judge if you are in the right position or if you are destined for more. Sometimes external forces present an opportunity to consider your options. Other times you are encouraged by friends, family, and mentors to reach further. Then again, maybe you are perfectly content with your present position for the long run. Your decision to advance your career should be based on your own internal dialog. Are you looking for more challenge, more responsibility, or are you seeking more attention, more prestige, more salary? There are good and bad reasons to advance your career. It is my hope that the good prevails. There is always room for better. So, consider that next position and take that leap. Your career is an opportunity to change the world.

43

Achieving Inner Peace

I am an optimistic person. I go out of my way to see the positive in life. Don't get me wrong, it is not as if I ignore or fail to consider the negativity in life, in fact I am a highly critical person. Rather I chose to focus on the positive in life to see the possibilities in the world around me. I have been asked how I can stay positive in times of hardship. As I have mentioned in previous posts, I am currently out of work. Yet as I think about being optimistic, I believe I can attribute my optimistic state to my own sense of inner peace.

Below I will share some of the ways I have learned to find and develop my sense of inner peace.

Knock your own socks off

When was the last time you did something that completely surprised yourself? When was the last time you were pleasantly shocked by something you did? Sometimes I think back about my life and career choices and cannot believe the risks that have paid off big. I took a risk at 17 to move out and move 400 miles from home to go to a community college. Because of that decision I met the future father of my son, got a college education, and found a career that I am passionate about to this day. Then there was a decision to apply for a position that I felt was way over my head. I was straight-out under qualified. Not only did I get the job, but I gained new skills that I never would have achieved if I never took that chance. Then there was the time I decided to host a golf tournament. It was the first time I ever did something that public and yet it was a resounding success! These surprise successes gave me a sense that I can take a risk and win big.

Face your own past

Do you let your past get in the way of your future? Would you rather ignore the pain and hurt of your younger self than face the difficult emotions as an adult? Life is messy. Everyone goes through tough times. Some people have had more than their fair share of pain and suffering. Even so, we cannot live life if we are busy hanging on to the pain. We need to let go so we can reach out and grasp new joys and happiness.

I had a very difficult childhood. There was poverty, the early death of my mother and father, an unstable household, different forms of abuse, neglect, and a lack of emotional support. I have come to terms with my past. I have worked out my feelings so that I see how my past is linked to my present, but my past does not control my daily life. I have found strength in the challenge I faced as a child. I realize that my past made me the person who I am today. I am very proud of the child I was and how she endured those experiences for it made me a resilient survivor who can adapt and thrive under pressure.

Forgive but never forget

It would be naive to say that you can forgive and forget all things. There are some hardships that can never be forgotten. But it is not healthy to hold onto negative feelings for something that can never be undone. We must find ways to forgive but it does not mean we need to forget.

Many people have hurts from our past, but there are also hurts that happen as an adult. There are three psychological pains, according to The Mind-Body Code - SoundsTrue.com, they are shame, abandonment, and betrayal.

It would be great to say that I have had nothing but warm and wonderful relationships with professionals in my field. The reality is that is not true. There were times when I have had to forgive people who should have known better. I know as people we are all facing our own demons or insecurities that cause people to act a certain way. So when I face someone who I felt has done me wrong, I learn to forgive, but I do not forget. I learn the lesson from the experience and move on.

Make your inner child proud

As I have stated above and in other posts, my childhood was no bowl of cherries. There were many missed opportunities as a child growing up. At the same time, I am reaching a point in my life where I need to present myself as a professional. So what can you do when you cannot go back and change time? You need to make time to play and have fun. I try not to take myself so seriously.

For example, I love the Muppets. When I was growing up my family did not always have a television and sometimes, we did not even have electricity or hot water in our house. So, I missed watching the Muppets on TV and I missed all the Muppet movies when they came to the theater. Therefore, when I found YouTube a few years ago, I spent a good portion of my time watching the Muppet Shows and songs and old movie clips. One of the funniest experiences I had was the first time I watched a Muppet movie with my young son. I am thankful that we can share an experience that is something I missed out on from my own childhood. It is something that is completely silly, but it warms my soul that I am honoring my inner child.

Slow your roll

Time keeps on ticking as the old song goes. When was that last time you took time to meditate, write a letter, journal, daydream, do some deep breathing, close your eyes and count to 10 (counting to 10 when you are mad does not apply), listen to music with your eyes closed, sit outside to feel the sunshine, walk barefoot in the grass, stare at the water or a beautiful landscape? These days we must plan everything, even time to daydream. I get my best ideas when I am staring off into space. When we are so busy that we have no down time, then we never get a chance to re-charge.

I have a friend who is a planner, her calendar is booked from sun up to sun down and everything in between. She once said that she wished everyone would just stop for one day. She is not making time for her own peace of mind in her plans.

As a single mother I understand the temptation to book every second of the day to get everything done. Even when I decided to go back to graduate school to complete my doctorate with a son entering Kindergarten, I knew I had to make time for being a mother, student, full-time professional, and a friend. As well, I knew I needed to take time for myself. Sure you cannot do everything you planned, but you need time to be yourself and love yourself in order to be there for everyone in your life. I journal to reflect on my life and meditate about major decisions in my life. It helps to take a step back as you plan your next project that will move your life forward.

Shine on
While I lived in New York City for graduate school it was hard to stop smiling and to not make eye contact with strangers. I remember one time I was riding the subway. I was thinking about how exciting and fun it was to be on a New York subway. I must have accidentally looked at a fellow passenger who thought I was trying to start a fight or something else. The passenger said, "What are you looking at?" in a threatening tone. "Geez", I thought to myself, "I am just being happy." I quickly shifted my gaze and tried hard not to make eye contact with anyone else. Since then I have learned an approach to dealing with strangers and others who are in a foul mood, but I do not let it bother me as much. I am not self-conscious of the fact that

I am positive and upbeat even when I do something as mundane as taking public transportation. Of course, I am not always in a positive mood, but when I am, I do not hide it. I now realize I get energized by sharing my joy with others.

Be generous

Do you remember a time when you truly helped someone else? Can you think of something you shared with someone else that made a difference? Did you give freely, without any prompting, offering something valuable with no strings attached? Giving to someone in need is a very rewarding experience. It is empowering to feel that you have abundance in your life that you can share with the world. There are many forms of abundance you can have such as wealth, knowledge, skills, health, connections, time, etc. It does not have to be a grand jester; it can be small. I am currently out of work, so I have free time on my hands. I have been helping another family with picking up their child from school. At first the family offered to pay me for my services. But the more I thought about it, I realized how nice it would have been if someone could have done that for me in my time of need, so I offer my services for free. The feeling of being generous is payment enough.

Show gratitude

When was the last time you thanked someone important in your life? Do you give credit to others in public? Do people you work with know how much you appreciate their work? There are many ways to show gratitude. It can be in a note, email, text, letter, or something else. When you express your gratitude you are valuing the role of that person in your life. Everyone wants to feel like they matter and that they made a difference in the world. By showing your appreciation, you are showing respect to that person. I always keep a box of Thank you notes in my desk at work. I am sure to send a thoughtful hand-written note to people who I work with who go the extra mile. For when it comes time for the next project, these are the people ready to help. I show appreciation for my staff because I value them as individuals. As well, I am humbled when I receive gratitude from my former staff and students. I am thrilled each time I receive a thank you email or card in the mail from a former student who is showing me gratitude. It is a beautiful circle!

Finding a sense of inner peace is different for each person. But I truly believe that finding room for inner peace is a short hop, skip, and a jump to finding personal success!

44

Getting Your Foot in the Door in Higher Education

I am often asked "How do you get your foot in the door for a job in student services on a college campus?" Below is some general information that I hope will be helpful for people interested in a career in student services at a California community college.

First, it is important to understand that student services encompass various functional areas along with instructional and operational services. Student services provide the interface between the institution and students necessary for navigation through the college-going experience. From the first time the student steps foot on campus or visits the college's website to the day the student graduates, the student relies on staff and faculty in these departments for day-to-day services. There is a solid foundation of student development theories and research behind student services that forms the basis for the operations and practices in these departments.

Second it is important to know the various areas of student services. Depending on the size of the college there can be various offices and departments within the area of student services such as Office of Admissions and Records, Assessment/Testing, Counseling, Outreach, Transfer, Veteran Services, Student Activities/Affairs/Development, Financial Aid, Disability Services, Health Services, Career/Workability, special programs such as EOPS/CARE, CalWORKs, Foster Youth/Kinship, Puente, Umoja, Honors, USDOE Title 3 or Title 5 HSI, AANAPISI, grant-funded programs, SSS, TRIO, Gear Up, Upward Bound, etc. Not all colleges have stand-alone offices or staff dedicated to these various areas, so it is important to familiarize yourself with the organization of the different divisions of student services at different colleges.

It is important to consider the differences between departments within student services. Perhaps you see a job announcement in Financial Aid and another job in Admissions and Records and another position in Outreach. Each job listing will have a different search committee looking at your application. These committees are made up of different groups of people who are usually from the department to which you are applying so your application should show that you are uniquely qualified for the position.

Go ahead and apply for multiple positions as long as you feel you are qualified for or interested in working in that area.

Please understand that working in Financial Aid versus Outreach versus Disability Services versus Veteran Services versus Transfer Services usually comes down to your personal experiences with these services, knowledge of federal and state regulations, understanding of how these departments interact together, and knowledge of the student population that the department serves.

You will also need to consider your own personal attributes and what you bring as a job candidate. It is a good idea to ask yourself a few personal questions to see if this is the right field for you.

Is your resume competitive and suitable for a career in student services?

As I mentioned in a previous post, there can be anywhere from 50 to 350 applicants for any given position. Make sure your resume lists relevant skills and experiences that relate to the job, include volunteer, student experiences, and personal information i.e. are you a military veteran, familiar with disability services, experienced filling out financial aid documents, a former community college student, aware of low-income student issues? Use the language and specific verbiage in the job announcement in your resume and cover letter if it applies to you.

Do you like public speaking?

At some point in your career in student services you will be asked to sit on a panel or to conduct trainings/workshops/informational sessions for small groups or in front of large audiences. You need to show that you can handle public speaking and enjoy making presentations.

Are you comfortable in an open office environment?

It is rare for staff members to have a traditional office with four walls. You might be stationed at a counter or desk in a cubicle with various staff members in proximity. There are constant interruptions, and you are often working on multiple projects at once. This open environment encourages collaboration, communication, and collegiality across departments.

Do you passionately believe that any student can be a success?

There are many reasons that students chose to attend a community college. Students come from every imaginable background. Part of your job is to support students to achieve their goals, whatever they might be. So you need to be energetic, enthusiastic, and positive in your interactions with students and the campus community.

Can you support and nurture a diverse student population?

There are students with learning disabilities, criminal backgrounds, economic hardships, language barriers, psychological challenges, physical and mental disabilities, and social barriers. You need to demonstrate your respect for diversity and your generosity for providing services and resources to all students.

It is important to be open to sharing knowledge and opportunities that promote our students' success.

Does working with the public and college personnel appeal to you?

In student services you will interact with a variety of people from college students to the public to professors to administrators to community organizations. In one day, you might deal with a concerned parent or a faculty member asking for assistance or a student in a crisis. You will need to be ready for constant social interactions with a wide range of constituencies.

Do you have specialized knowledge/experience relevant to a particular department?

Were you a transfer student, in a honors program, a military veteran, a student with disabilities, a student leader, a campus tour guide, a student athlete, a re-entry student, a single parent, in EOPS, on state aid, a community college student, in a student retention program like Puente, Umoja, or Upward Bound? Were you a recipient of financial aid or scholarships or have experience working on campus as a student? Your cover letter should demonstrate that you can relate to the students in community college. As well, it is important that you are socially aware of the issues facing community college students.

Are you comfortable with a cyclical calendar and repetitive questions?

There is a set pattern of processes, timelines, and projects on a college campus. Every year begins with the rush of students asking the same questions in a million different ways. In the middle of the term, students are anxious about mid-terms and projects. Then at the end of the year there are students getting ready to move on or they are getting ready to continue their planning for the next year or next goal. At times it feels like there is not enough time in the day and other times it feels like you are in the dullest of doldrums with very little to fill up your day. You will need patience and creativity to distinguish your work schedule. Each day is something different, yet each day is an opportunity to positively affect a student's life.

Ultimately, I hope that you take these questions into consideration as you decide whether or not to apply for a position in student services. It takes extreme perseverance to land that first interview. Your introspection now will be good preparation for getting your foot in the door. With this personal reflection, you should be able to hone your resume and cover letter to express your interests in a way that makes your application stand out. It is your answers to these questions that should help you make your decision.

In the end, it comes down to knowing yourself and knowing the college. Apply broadly and apply often. You will need to consider various offices and departments to get your foot in the door. Once a part of the college, there is opportunity for growth and development to specialize your career.

Here's to making your passion your career!

45

One Truly Unfortunate Interview

This interview happened a couple of years ago. It was a final interview for a position I really wanted. Not only would it mean a promotion and hefty raise in salary, but it also meant moving to a place that would be closer for my son to be near his dad.

It was about an hour by plane. I had flown there a few weeks before for the first-level interview without incident. So, for the final interview I planned to do the same flight plan and rent the car just as I did the first time.

Anytime you fly in for an interview, it is an adventure. For me, this interview would go down in infamy.

My taxi was scheduled to pick me up at 5:00am the morning of the interview. My flight was scheduled for 9:00am so there would be plenty of time to get to the airport. The problems began when my alarm failed to wake me up. Instead of waking up at 3:30am in time to take a shower and get dressed, I was awoken by the taxi driver calling to tell me I had 5 minutes to get outside for the pickup. I barely had time to toss all my makeup in a carry-on bag and to dress in my interview suit.

Instead of taking a shower and getting ready in the comfort of my own house, I was brushing my teeth in the women's restroom at the airport. Not only that but I forgot my deodorant. I hastily applied my makeup using the unflattering florescent lighting. Of course, I had no way to wash my hair for the interview. To top it off, I noticed that the shirt I had picked out was not freshly laundered, in fact there was an obvious stain on the front. I tried to get the stain out with water, but it made the stain worse. As I rushed to the gate to board the plane, there was an announcement that there was a delay to the flight. The plane left an hour after the scheduled time.

Fortunately, I arrived at my destination with time to get the rental car and drive to the interview location. Unfortunately, when it came time to pay for the rental car, my only credit card was declined. I had been interviewing for months in various locales, flying in and out of different parts of the state. My credit card was simply too close to the limit so there was enough credit for the rental, but not the deposit. I did not realize that the rental company I was trying to use had to hold a large deposit. So, I stood there at the rental counter and called my credit card company to inquire about a credit line increase. I HAD to rent a car to get to the interview! Lucky for me, an agent witnessed my dilemma and informed me about a discount car rental company down the hall that did not hold a large deposit. I was able to rent the car using the tip from the agent.

I finally got on the road with one hour to get to the interview location which was about 40 miles from the airport. In a stroke of good luck, I got there without a hitch.

When I got to the campus, I was informed that the interview time had changed because the campus was having their accreditation site visit that day and it was running off schedule. I needed to sit in the lobby until the college president was free. I sat and waited. I waited for over one hour. The whole time I was waiting, I wondered if I had time to sneak away to the Cosmetology Department for a quick shampoo and blow dry. Nope, no such luck. I was going into this interview as is.

When the college president was finally available, we sat down for the interview. I was grilled for an hour by the college president and two faculty members about every rule and regulation pertaining to the areas of responsibility for the position. I had prepared extensively and had answers for many questions, but it was still grueling.

Chapter 45

I thought the interview was over, but it wasn't. I was informed that there would be a second part to the interview which was an open forum with the college community. Yikes! I was escorted to a hall where there was a podium and a mic with an audience waiting for me. As I took my place behind the podium, I wondered if anyone would be able to see the stain on my shirt or notice that my hair was unwashed. It felt like torture standing there wondering if anyone saw my shoddy makeup job.

At the open forum I was asked to tell the crowd a little about myself and why I wanted the position. Suddenly, my insecurities vanished, because I wanted to show the crowd that I was the best person for the job. After my presentation, the audience had an opportunity to ask me questions. It lasted about 45 minutes in total. It was the first time I had done an open forum for an interview, but I felt like I did a good job.

After the open forum was over, I was escorted back to the president's office. The college president informed he would be making a final decision about the position that afternoon.

I did not think I would get the job. It felt like too much had gone wrong. I am not a superstitious person, but it felt like there were too many bad signs. I woke up late. I nearly missed my flight. I had no time to take a shower. My hair and makeup were messy. There was a stain on my shirt. I almost couldn't get a rental car. The interview was delayed because of the accreditation visit. The open forum was a complete surprise, and I did not feel prepared. How could this possibly go right?

Well, believe it or not, I got the job!

What I realized later is that if you are focused, you can overcome obstacles that might seem outside your control. From the moment I woke up that morning, I knew had to make that interview happen. Because I was late, the whole day was go, go, go! I had no time for doubt! I could have given up at many points in the day, but I didn't. It paid off in the end. I always tell my students to never give up on yourself. If you believe in yourself, anything is possible. Focus on your goals and make your goals happen. While I will always remember this interview as the most embarrassing interview of my life, it is also one of my most proud moments.

46

Wowing the Crowd with Your Interview Presentation

You finally get 'the call' or 'the email'. They want to interview you. Great news! You set a time and date for the big event. You find out you need to prepare a presentation about a major issue facing the institution. Then you are informed that you will be completing a written assignment as well. Now all you need to do is get ready to wow the crowd.

The first-level interview for a management position at a community college is intense. There is a panel interview, meaning there can be anywhere from 5 to 15 people interviewing you at once. There may even be an open forum portion that is open to anyone at the college. The interview questions are jam-packed with various types of questions which typically include at least one scenario question as well as general get-to-know-you type of questions. There is usually a time limit for the whole process, so closely monitor how much time you spend on the questions. And since it is a regimented process, all candidates are asked the same pre-set questions.

The good news is that your application was selected out of possibly 100's of others. Even so, at the initial interview, you could be up against over a dozen other candidates hoping to secure that open position. Your presentation and writing sample can give you the edge you need to make it to the next round.

The presentation and writing sample are two pieces of the overall picture of your interview. Sometimes people are concerned that someone might "steal" their ideas/materials/strategies/outcomes/goals or that the interview is going to provide free solutions for the college's issues.

The first-level interview is a process of learning about various candidates in a comprehensive manner. The interview materials that you produce are simply another way for the interview panel to learn about your skills, abilities, and knowledge.

What is important is the amount of work that you put into the details of your material. Below are some general tips to help you wow the crowd:

Use PowerPoint

This is a professional presentation, and your technical skills are under scrutiny. Follow the general rules of using PowerPoint but use it even if you only have a 10-minute presentation. You can decide to print handouts, but it is not necessary.

Grammar Counts

It is an academic environment and there will be professors on the interview panel. Take care because someone will be making a note of any errors.

Know Your College

Nothing irks a panel more than getting the name of the college wrong. Know how the college is referred to by people who work there. Be careful when using acronyms since not all colleges refer to the various offices/committees/processes with the same terminology as other colleges or industries. Try to get a feel for the college via the college's website. Make references to the college current events and/or telltale identifiers. Is it the 60th Anniversary of the college or did the college just win the state championship in football? Include college symbols and pictures from their website in your material.

Practice, practice, practice

Check the time of your presentation and ask someone to check your slides for any typos. If you have not written anything for a while, practice writing for the writing sample. You will have about 20 minutes to answer a prompt. You should have enough time to write a couple of paragraphs. It does not present well to be skimpy on the writing sample.

Greet the Panel

The panel is made up of managers, staff, faculty, community members, and students. These are people who may or may not be under your direct supervision. You may even know people on the panel. There may even be the person who you will be replacing on the committee. Treat everyone with respect and show appreciation for having the opportunity to interview. Even if you know people on the panel, greet the panel as a group.

Talk it Up

Every candidate is asked the exact same questions in the preliminary interview. As well, some colleges do not allow the panel to ask follow-up questions. Expand on your skills and experience as much as possible if it is relevant to the position. Do not assume that panel will refer to your resume or application materials when it comes time to rate you as a candidate. Quite the opposite. For some reason, it has become a practice that a committee will tell the candidate that if they fail to mention any pertinent information during the interview, the committee cannot include it in the evaluation. For example, imagine you have a doctorate degree, you mention the degree on your application, cover letter, and your resume, but if you fail to mention it during the interview, the committee will not include your doctorate in the evaluation. It makes ZERO sense, but I have seen it happen.

Have Fun

The panel members might be interviewing candidates all week or back-to-back over a few days. It is important that you bring energy, enthusiasm, and excitement to the presentation.

The panel is not looking for someone who thinks they have all the answers but someone who will be a great person to work with at the college. Show the panel the reason why you would like to work at their college. Lastly, don't forget to make good eye contact, speak clearly, smile, and try to enjoy the experience.

There are many components to the first-level interview at a community college. Many hours of preparation have gone into the process by the interview panel to find the best candidate. Have respect for the process and do your part by bringing your best self to the interview. Then you will be ready to wow the crowd.

47

Mentors are Immortal

Everyone struggles with their sense of mortality. When disasters strike, the delicateness of our physical existence is thrown smack dab in our collective face. Whether natural or human-made, these disasters force us to take stock of our lives. I live in the San Francisco Bay Area where there has been national attention over the last two weeks because of the passing of Robin Williams and due to the largest earthquake to strike the area in 25 years. These were two major events that touched many people in different ways. While the earthquake is something that can be explained using science, the passing of Robin Williams was inexplicable, sudden, and left many unanswered questions because it came because of his own doing.

The passing of Robin Williams made me think about his lifetime's work and what made him so special to so many. Everyone agrees his work was legendary. In my opinion, two stellar acting roles that immediately spring to mind were from the movies "Good Will Hunting" and "Dead Poet's Society". His work in these movies exemplify his broad emotional range and acting skills. Another reason these movie roles stand out in my memories of Robin Williams is because education was the premise in these movies and as someone fascinated by the field of education, the roles resonated with my personal journey. These roles are more poignant now as I have been fortunate to have a career in education myself. In these movies he played the role of a mentor, someone dedicated to students and to their success. His loss made me to think back on some of the wonderful mentors that I have had over the years who have passed on as well. In these roles, Robin Williams was so spectacular because he presented himself as a man of strength, courage, and wisdom in addition to possessing a sense of humor that was out of this world - a rare combination. It is no wonder that he will always be remembered as a legend.

I consider my mentors to be legends as well. Having a great mentor can be the best thing in your life when you are first starting out in the world, be it in college, at work, or as a leader in the community. Mentors are there to give advice, hear you out, share their stories, push you to new heights, and to be a touchstone as you move forward with your goals.

So, what happens when our mentors pass on?

Losing a mentor can feel just like the loss of a family member, depending on the closeness of the relationship. I have had a few mentors pass away over the last few years. While they may not be with me in the physical world, I feel that the impact of my mentors is in a sense immortal. We carry on our mentor's life in what we make of ourselves. I carry on in the memory of my mentors without a doubt.

One of my first mentors was a total anti-hero, rascal, and rebel. She was a curmudgeon and misanthrope if ever there was one. She was a thin, wiry, elderly African American lady who was completing the tail end of her career. Her personality belied her career as a counselor at a community college working in student services. There were many instances of eye rolling whenever she got on a tirade during a department staff meeting. Yet on the other side of one of her longwinded diatribes, there was usually a nugget of absolute solid gold. While we did not hold a formal relationship as mentor/protégé, I would go to her for advice on a regular basis. The most intense and deep conversations we had about student success were sitting in her office. After breaking thru her tough exterior, she made me feel like I was doing the most important job in the world. When she found out I was pregnant, I can vividly recall the sparkle of joy in her eyes. We had such memorable conversations that I used these discussions as the basis for my doctoral dissertation research more than 10 years later. I remember one time she shared with me that one of her biggest regrets in life was that she did not attend a historically black college as an undergraduate. Here was someone who touched the lives of countless students each year in her work, yet her college choice was something she regretted all her life. I cannot explain the thrill and honor I experienced years later when I was able to help my first student complete the university application to a historically black college. When my mentor told me, she received news she had cancer, I was in shock and disbelief. Within two months she was gone. She worked pretty much to her last living day, but the sickness struck quickly. I think of her often. I try to listen to my students and staff as intensely as she did during all those conversations we had in her office.

I had another mentor who was the life of the party. He would bring his sense of humor to the driest, dullest meetings and make his data analytics presentations come alive. Every day he wore a Hawaiian shirt and a smile a mile wide. He was a numbers guy who should have been working for the government, but he settled for working in a research office at my community college. I loved the way he would toss out facts and figures like they were the easiest ideas to comprehend. Yet he put concepts out there so anyone could see how it all fit together to form the bigger picture. Because of him I learned about forecasting and projections and how to think about the future for strategic planning. He introduced me to the notion of being a futurist. I got introduced to work being done focused on the next 20 years in higher education. He made the future look exciting, amazing, and better than anything one could imagine. There was this one time I remember, we had to drive to a meeting taking place about an hour away from campus. We decided to carpool. In the car was myself, my college president, and my mentor. Under a different circumstance I would have felt intimidated or left out of the conversation. Instead, my mentor started in with the jokes and stories about living in Hawaii, and asking me about my work, and before I knew it, we reached the destination of the meeting. My good friend and mentor made everyone feel a part of something wonderful. His illness lasted over a year or so, and everyone knew he was sick. Even so, he was a great person who lived life to the fullest. I remember his enthusiasm for our work the most. I think of him now that some of the initiatives he worked on have become part of the state legislation. He was always looking at the long view, so I do that in my work as well.

When legends pass on, their impact and stories remain. The people who were close to them will never forget them. Their spirit lives on in our hearts and in our work. I have been touched by the kindness and generosity of the mentors I have had in my life. Now that I have reached a leadership position in my career, I feel obligated to return the favor. While it is tough losing a wonderful mentor, who is a close friend, it is now time for me to step into their shoes to offer for others what I have received.

It can be hard to lose a mentor because you never quite stop needing a mentor. I continue to seek out mentors, yet I am more often left without that touchstone as I move along in my career path. It is times like this that I am reminded how lucky I have been to have been so close to the greats. While these legends passed years ago, their presence is as strong today as it was when first we met. For this reason, I believe that mentors are immortal.

48

Getting your First Full-time Job in Student Services

The year was 2007, there were over 275 applicants for the position I wanted and somehow, I got the job! It felt especially triumphant given that this new position would mean returning to the place of my upbringing. It meant returning to the same town where I was born and raised. I left town when I was 17 years old. Back then I was ashamed of how I grew up, being poor and from a dysfunctional and broken family. I was an underachieving student who barely graduated high school. I faced an uncertain future. Yet, now I was returning home as a manager in student services at the local community college. The same college that I used to escape to when I ditched classes so I could waste countless hours watching cable tv because I did not have a tv or cable at my house.

My new position was coveted by many, yet I managed to beat the competition. Winning this promotion meant I had the necessary education, experience, and knowledge to advance in my career. This event was a sweet professional victory full of significance to my personal growth and development as a leader in higher education administration. Reaching this victorious milestone was a result of a journey that began with my first position in student services many years earlier.

There are 116 community colleges in the state of California. The oldest college is over 100 years old, and the newest college just opened its doors a few years ago. The colleges serve over 2 million students, many students are low income or the first in their family to pursue higher education. At each campus there are three distinct operational divisions. These divisions are instruction, operations, and student services. At each campus there are on average 200 staff positions, with roughly half the positions being in student services. That means that there are over 11,000 positions in student services statewide and currently 1,200 positions are open. To fill one of those staff positions, there can be anywhere from 50 to 300 applicants. With an average of 175 applicants for each position, that means over 200,000 applicants are vying for these positions. With the competition throughout the state, how can one hope to get a position? What follows is some of my own experience working in student services at a community college.

Over the life of my career, I have worked at six different community colleges and five four-year universities. As well, I have hired and interviewed applicants for positions in administration, faculty, staff, athletics, volunteers, interns, and have evaluated hundreds of applications. Applying and hiring for any job takes time, effort, energy, research, and faith. There is the faith on the part of the applicants that they are the best candidate for the job and faith on the part of the institution that the candidate will have the support and resources to be a success. I have been on the applicant side and the hiring manager side many times.

As a hiring manager, I often wonder if every person who applies for a position has really considered whether they are truly the best person for the job, especially for a job in student services at a community college. When I am hiring, I am looking for the best. This is because I believe that the students in community college deserve the very best. Why do I feel this way? For one, it is because I used to be a community college student myself. Second, I believe that someone working in student services at a community college must have experience, knowledge, and passion for the work that is being done. Third, I feel that people in these positions must demonstrate that they value, respect, and understand that any student can be a success no matter what their personal background or their educational history. So, with these kinds of expectations, how did I manage to obtain my first entry-level position in student services?

As an applicant I had a tough time breaking into the community college system. I completed my Master of Arts degree in student personnel administration from an Ivy League institution, an internship in student services working with inner-city students, and I was a former community college student myself. I naively thought finding a position in student services would be easy. Was I wrong! In my first go-round, I applied to over 250 positions before I got my first interview.

In the interim, I wondered if I would ever land a job in student services. I originally got interested in this type of work because of the experience I had as a community college student. The services at the college provided me with the knowledge and support I needed to transfer to a university and earn a bachelor's degree. I would never forget the confidence boost I felt the day I received my first acceptance letter from the universities where I applied. From that moment on I saw the community college as a place of limitless possibilities. For someone like me to be able to turn my prospects around after only two short years of study, I knew I wanted to have a career working for the community college system. My mentors and college professors encouraged me to pursue a career as a faculty member. While I did not want to disappoint my mentors, I felt that what made the most difference in my education were all the supportive staff members in student services and the faculty who went out of their way to teach me how to navigate my way around the institution from financial aid to college exploration to student life. In looking at the big picture, I even fantasized about being the president of my community college one day. So, at the age of 19 I knew my career path would involve working on a college campus in some form or fashion.

During my initial job search, what I failed to consider was that there are millions of former community college students and university students who have a passion for student services just like me. In fact, other applicants had prior student services experience through working on campus because of work-study, student work, volunteering, internships, and student involvement in such areas as admissions, outreach, club officer positions, student government, and teacher assistantships. There are thousands of community college students working on college campuses throughout the state. They leverage that experience into a career at the community college. Not only are these applicants passionate about the community college system, but they have personal experience with many of the services and programs at the college as well. Sadly, for me, I was not lucky enough to have any experience working at the community college from when I was a student. When I was a college student, I did not even understand how work study worked. As an undergraduate, I was slogging away in customer service jobs. At first, I felt like I was at a disadvantage once again.

Even so, I have been fortunate to have landed various positions in different student service areas including university transfer services, assessment/testing, admissions and records, orientation services, EOPS/CalWORKs, diversity programs, financial aid, tutoring services, and outreach services throughout my career. I have competed with hundreds of applicants at each turn.

One reason that there is such a high number of applicants for each position is because the colleges use electronic application systems, and all the jobs are publicly listed online. In the state of California, all public community college positions are listed on the CCC Registry website, www.cccregistry.org. As well jobs are listed on college websites and in specialty recruiting publications online such as the Chronicle of Higher Education, www.chronicle.com. As someone looking for a career in student services, it can feel impossible to get your foot in the door. But the career field provides countless rewards and satisfaction in serving students to help them meet their personal and academic goals.

Working in student services at a community college is a vital part of serving the future success of our students, local communities, the workforce, academia, and all of humanity. As well, as you think about applying for these positions, consider that these colleges have a long, proud history and are a critical part of this country's success as a nation.

My passion for working in student services in community college stems from my personal college experience but what I have told is a common story that is shared by many others in this career field. It is a field that is filled with professionals dedicated to the success of our college students. While this essay may include what is thought to be too much personal information, it is important to understand that our students face similar experiences that should be the foundation for our work in the field of student services. It is for these and countless other reasons that our students deserve the best. These positions are as important to the students as they are to the professionals who choose to make the field of student services their career. It is my hope to underscore the importance of these positions in meeting the mission of the community college system.

As I look back on the pride I felt in landing that position many years ago, I am reminded that there are many others who are just beginning their journey into the field of student services. I would encourage anyone considering this field to reflect on your own life experiences. What are your own strengths and what fuels your desire to serve students at the community college level? Have you considered how your education and skills match the positions in student services? If you have very little experience from your formal education or paid positions, then I would encourage you to volunteer, intern, or to further your education with a master's or doctoral degree in a related field such as Counseling, Student Personnel Administration, Psychology,

Public Administration, Higher Education Administration, or a field listed in the job description under "Minimum Qualifications".

Many entry-level positions list an associate in arts degree with years of experience to be considered. When I first applied, I had my master's degree and one year of experience. Do not let the level of your education prevent you from applying for the job. If you are not sure about applying but you have the passion for the work, then go for it! As they say on the Forums on the Chronicle of Higher Education website http://chronicle.com/forums/index.php/board,26.0.html, "Apply for the Damn Job." It is a great career, and it starts with that first step.

I wish everyone all the success on the journey. Great things await you! You never know, you could become a college president someday.

49

Positivity Starts Inside Our Self

The year is 2014. I got fired. I lost my job. Losing your job is one of the most stressful events you can experience. People tout how critical it is to stay positive.

But how do you stay positive when the bills keep coming, there is no next paycheck, you interview like crazy but there is no job offer? At some point, you begin to wonder if it is time to change career fields. Still, I am staying positive.

How do I stay positive? I do it by reminding myself that I have overcome worse than this before.

I found out I would be losing my job about 6 months ago. That is the crazy thing about working in higher education, everything moves slower, even a layoff. Since I received my "pink slip" notice, I have applied to dozens of positions in my field. There have been tons of first and second level interviews over the last three months. I have been a "finalist" 5 times. I was 100% certain I would find something by July. But so far, no job offers in hand.

With no job in sight, I let the lease on my rental house run out. I moved my family, my son, and my dog from our 3-bedroom house and large backyard. I downsized to a small apartment. Moving is also considered one of life's most stressful events. Still, I remain positive.

How so?

First off, losing my job will not define me as a person. My life has been filled with turbulence, struggle, success, and survival. These life experiences define me, not my work. I draw strength from memories of my mom. My mother came alone from Mexico when she was 16 years old. She did not speak any English and she came by herself with no money or education or skills. I also draw strength from my dad. My father served in the Air Force for four years and became a lawyer on his own. My sisters and my brother also give me strength. I have four siblings and we all have had varying degrees of luck in life. Sadly, my mother left this earth when she was just 37 years old. I was 12 years old at the time. Then my father passed away when I was 29 years old. Both of my parents died penniless and without a home to call their own. Losing my parents early taught me the value of making your life count no matter how long or little you live.

When I landed my first full-time dream job, I was 28 years old. I was doing something I loved at a place I really loved, with people that would end up becoming lifelong mentors and friends. A month into my new job I found out my position was being eliminated due to state budget cuts. A month after that I found out I was pregnant about to become a single mother. I was laid off and ended up homeless, on public assistance, and as a newly single mother I gave birth to a healthy bouncing baby boy. How did I manage? I counted on family and friends for help. From this experience I learned that I needed to think about the future for my son and not to dwell on feeling sorry for myself.

Then there was the memory of the time I got my first management position. It felt like a dream come true. Here I was a single mother from humble beginnings, but I had found a well-paying position that brought with it a sense of respect, authority, and leadership. I felt like I had the perfect opportunity to develop and flourish as a professional. It was in this position that my direct supervisor, a Latina executive with a resume like my own, shattered my confidence one day. A strong Latina professional who I admired told me to my face that I was not "Latina" enough, that I was too tall as a woman, that I was too assertive, and that I intimidate people. This woman who was my boss, told me I should sit down when I address students to appear more approachable. This was the first and last time I allowed someone to speak to me in such a demeaning and derogatory way. What I learned here is that I don't need to change myself to be successful and that I should be proud of myself no matter what anyone else says.

These lessons have been hard to experience, but they are my lived experience. Even so, I have pressed on. A few years ago, I completed my doctorate degree. As well, I continue to attend leadership seminars where my hopes for my career path have been validated and encouraged by professionals in my field. Over the years, I have received wonderful mentorship and professional acknowledgements that have instilled in me a sense of pride, honor, and respect for my work and the path that brought me to my perspective on leadership in higher education.

So, this last time when I was told I would be facing unemployment I had new acquaintances express sincere concern about my future. They wanted to know how I was going to handle it. For me, I put it all into perspective. I have 12 years of experience in my field now. I have my doctorate in hand. I have my savings that will help. I am not homeless, for now. I am healthy. My son is 10 years old and old enough to understand a little better the urgency to downsize. Yes, it is a difficult time, but I am staying positive.

I am reaching out to my network of friends and former colleagues. I am perfecting my resume. I am going back and reading my letters of recommendation to see how others see my skills and experience. I am exploring career options in closely related fields. I am mentoring others about job searching and career exploration. I am imagining the great accomplishments I will achieve in my next position. Most importantly, I am surrounding myself with positive people.

Mainly, I keep busy. I listen to music that is uplifting and upbeat. I am doing things I never had time to do before, like write and read. I am enjoying not having a job for now. I know that eventually something will come my way.

Staying positive is not about being oblivious to the negativity in your life. It is about drawing strength from the challenges you have overcome in your life. I believe in myself because my faith has been tested multiple times and I have come out thriving. I know I can count on myself because I have the skills, knowledge, and experience to be successful. My strength comes from knowing I can survive. For me, there is no other option. In the meanwhile, I recall what my father would tell us children (and himself no doubt) when we were complaining and whining about our unfortunate life, "This too shall pass".

50

Perceiving Strength in Others

There is a common saying in the world of work when it comes to hiring/promotions/assignments, better to hire the devil we know versus the devil we don't know. The basis for this saying is the idea that the unknown is scarier than the known. Knowing the faults of the "devil" we are most familiar with must somehow be better than the potential faults of the "devil" we do not know.

The "devil" who is known might be a former employee, internal candidate, a close personal referral, or other highly recommended candidate. This "devil" is someone with whom his or her faults, trouble spots, questionable previous employment experiences, uneven job performance, quirky disposition, bad personal relationships, etc. are all somehow more acceptable than the unknown.

The "devil" who is unknown is usually an external candidate, unfamiliar or outside our close network of peers/colleagues, or a wild card candidate from outside the industry. This "devil" is someone with whom he or she is a blank slate. The possibilities about this "devil's" job performance are endless, be they good and bad.

So, why is it so easy to assume the worst? Why all this fear? Making a hiring mistake is expensive, time consuming, disheartening, and disappointing. We all want to avoid a bad hire! But we cannot let fear of the unknown stymie a hiring process.

Granted, fear of the unknown is natural. The challenge is to get over the inherent bias that often happens in close-knit environments which leads many to go with the familiar and the safe options. The halo effect is real and causes hiring committees to value similarities over valuable experience and skills for the actual position. Instead, we must look at the opportunity to hire as a chance to make a positive decision based on facts, not fear.

Instead of looking at job candidates based on the deficit model (what skills/experience they lack), how about evaluating candidates based off their strengths (what value can they bring)?

The candidates are not the "devil". The "devil" is fear. It is up to all of us to stare fear in the face and to remove it from the hiring process. Clearly, the hiring process is not a game for the weak of heart. But by naming the "devil" by its correct name, we can remove its power. Persist on, brave soldiers!

51

Making Positive Decisions as a Manager

Holding a position as a manager means you are constantly making decisions. There are decisions that are major, life changing ones and small, minor, insignificant ones. When you are in a position of leadership, your decisions can impact the organization, the community, the operations, and countless people who look to you to make good decisions.

So, it is interesting that when faced with making these decisions, there is no magic bullet to figuring out how to make your decisions besides your own intuition and the law.

I used to work with a supervisor who would warn us managers "Every day you guys make decisions that could get me fired. So, don't get me fired!"

It is true every decision can have a vital impact on the institution, but a true leader should provide a framework for the decision-making process so the management team can uphold the shared visions and goals of the CEO and the organization.

There are moments when you have time to mull over your decisions and then there are occasions when a decision must be made in the blink of an eye or split minute. In these moments, what you do can shape the rest of your career and your life, each time, and every day! That is why managers supposedly get paid "the big bucks."

Below are some tips to help you figure out how to make decisions:

Be Kind

No matter the situation, it serves no purpose to be anything but kind in the face of a major decision. Perhaps someone has come to you for a raise or request for promotion. This request may be impossible to fulfill or there may be no resources or perhaps the person making the request is a terrible, pompous, backstabber. Either way, my rule of thumb is to be kind and explain the decision to the person so there are no hurt feelings.

Have Fun

Perhaps you are presented with a request to support something silly or frivolous or unusual but socially engaging. I have seen my colleagues quash perfectly acceptable ideas simply on the notion that the organization should not lower its standards with something less than traditional or professional. Having fun with employees brings the team together. As well, it takes courage and faith to present new ideas to the management. Innovation and creativity should be rewarded, within reason.

Live with No Regrets

Belief that your decision is right and based on sound reasoning is essential as a manager. Often you can hear multiple opinions of the best course of action to take to address a problem, but the final decision rests on your plate. Some decisions are too big for one person to handle. If you need help, ask for it. If you are too scared to decide, decide anyway. But you need to stand behind your actions. Considering whether the course of action you take will lead to regret is a good way to gauge on what to do.

Trust Your Gut

Professional development seminars, graduate courses, books, and articles harp on the use of intuition in decision making. In other words, you need to be able to trust your gut. But few people are well versed in being able to understand what that means.

It means being in tune with your emotional and physiological reactions to certain situations. Your body sends signals to you about how to respond your environment. These signals must not be ignored. Part of having true emotional intelligence is knowing your own emotional states. Paying attention to these emotions will help you learn to read your own gut reactions. Overtime you will learn to trust your gut more and more.

Make Your Future-Self Proud

We all have an idea of where we want our career to go in the future. What would your future-self tell your present-day-self about the choices you are making? There is a saying that hindsight is 20/20. Well, instead of always looking backwards, practice looking into the future. Are the decisions you are making going to help you reach the goals you have for your future career? Consider a new project or assignment under discussion, if that is something that will help you move your career forward, then you should find a way to involve yourself.

Be Brave

It can be tempting to make no decision at all in some instances. Some managers become masters of passing the buck. Decision by indecision. This often happens in large organizations where there are several people who might or might not decide to get an idea off the ground. Instead of passing the buck, be the one to decide and end it for once and for all.

Surprise Yourself

I cannot emphasize enough the importance of trying new things or going down untraveled roads. Perhaps there is no one backing a new idea at the organization. You can take the idea from the wayside to the next level. Take the reins and let the horses run free occasionally. You might be surprised where it takes you.

Act with Love

There should always be good intentions behind the thinking of the decisions you must make. After all, being in a management position is a privilege that is not available to everyone. While sometimes it can be fun to fantasize about what it would be like to throttle someone with a soul crushing decision denying that request from that one person who just makes your skin crawl. But be compassionate. You do not know the reason that person is such a pain in the neck, the personal issues that make that person the way they are. My dad used to use the term to give one "the benefit of the doubt". There should be a basic love of humanity or love of the civility or love of law and order or some other kind of love that is from a place of goodness for every decision that needs to be made.

Cause No Harm

Will the decision you make cause harm in anyway? Harm can take many shapes at an organization. Harm can affect resources, facilities, reputation, standing, status, morale, staff, community, relationships, and much more. At the end of the day, the manager is responsible for the sustainability of the organization. Nothing done and no one decision should lead to the dismantling or destruction of the entity. Then the decisions made should be in relation to the sustainability of the organization. Interestingly, there can be many interpretations of what might or might not cause actual harm to the institution. Therefore, for this consideration, the first and foremost concern should be about the welfare, health and safety of people and then go from there.

Know Your Weaknesses

We all have a sense of the type of manager we are and the type of manager we would like to be. It takes a strong sense of self to realize your own shortcomings and areas of weakness.

For example, I know that I am not the most patient person in the world. I am often very enthusiastic and eager to get new projects off the ground. I am also painfully aware of how long it takes for projects to take root and to gain the support of multiple constituencies. Therefore, I work to be more conscientious of taking time to build support and understanding of my ideas when I need to make a major decision about a new project.

In the end, every decision you make should be well thought out and with care. I have learned a great deal about the power of making good decisions. Some of the best decisions I have made have involved hiring decisions that will have a lasting impact on the organization. As well, I have seen the result of making poor decisions. I once made a terrible decision that resulted in me losing my job. Some decisions give us pride and others make us cringe. But taking time to think about and strategize about our decisions builds knowledge and strength to ensure that our decisions are the best for your professional development and your organization.

There are many reasons for things that happen in our life, but we must not downplay our own power to make good decisions.

52

Nurturing the Body Politic

The year was 2018. It is a year that will go down in history as one of the most tumultuous years in United States political history. It is also a year that I will always remember with fondness as it was the year I first ran for political office.

In 2018, I put everything on the line and ran for the statewide position of State Superintendent of Public Instruction to lead the Department of Education at the state-level. While I finished in third place in the primary election, I did learn a great deal about the political process.

I will share a few tidbits of what I learned as a first-time political candidate.

ANYONE CAN (AND SHOULD) RUN FOR POLITICAL OFFICE

Before I ran for office, I imagined that a person needed to have a paid political campaign staff, a professional campaign manager, a press secretary, a marketing guru, a full-time graphic designer, and millions of dollars just to get your name on the ballot. The great news is that all of that is false. I thought you had to be a perfect candidate. But the reality is, there is NO perfect candidate! All a person needs to do is pay a filing fee and get a minimum number of signatures and be 18 years old and be eligible to vote. In my case, I simply needed to pay the filing fee and get 100 valid signatures of registered voters to get my name on the election ballot. Totally doable!

EXPECT A LAWSUIT

Lawsuits happen for any reason. I received a notice about a lawsuit over my ballot designation. A candidate gets to use three words that will go under his/her name on the official ballot. I wanted to use "Teacher/Educational Administrator" and was facing a lawsuit over the use of the term "teacher." Who was the one suing me? One of the other candidates running for the position. Was the lawsuit covered in the news or on social media? Nope! The Fair Political Practices Commission (FPPC) has a policy on terms and designations that can/cannot be used. In the end, instead of litigating over the term "teacher", I changed the designation to read "Instructor/Educational Administrator." None of the candidates on the ballot had ever been a full-time tenured teacher. I had experience as a substitute teacher. Believe it or not, there are paid consultants that charge thousands of dollars just to come up with ballot designations!

STRIKE WHILE THE IRON'S HOT

There are numerous support groups for first time candidates. There are groups for women, people of color, radical, young, democrat, republican, liberal, progressive, conservative, libertarian, etc. If you learn more about these groups, you come to meet people who have been thinking about running for political office for years. Groups have members who are complete experts on the political process, yet they are too scared to run for office. I say, you need to strike while the iron is hot. There is never going to be a "perfect" time to run. I learned about the office I was running for from the Secretary of State and Wikipedia. The time was right. There was no incumbent. The position would not be up for election for another four years. I was eminently qualified. I was technically unemployed at the time, so I was available to focus 100% on the campaign. As well, the tumultuous political climate meant people were looking for different and first-time candidates with heart and determination. Perfect!

SOCIAL MEDIA TRANSCENDS PHYSICAL BOUNDARIES AND BARRIERS

Being connected online provided support, resources, networks, information, and collaborations that made running a campaign simultaneously easy and challenging. I could send out 7,000 email communications at the touch of a button, which I did often. Using Twitter, Facebook, Instagram, YouTube, LinkedIn, and blogs, I was communicating across the state of California and across the country with ease. I received interview offers, invitations to local and community events, posted videos and daily updates. My media campaign did not cost me a penny, yet I was able to get my campaign to reach others far and wide. I was pleasantly surprised when I received a call one day inviting me to attend an event in Washington, DC. All things are possible with social media. My political campaign simply would not have been possible without social media. Social media helps to level the playing field.

PRESS AND THE HOLY GRAIL – ENDORSEMENTS

The major press outlets and the political endorsement process is not what it may seem to the casual observer. I learned that there are candidates who received endorsements from every major newspaper in the state and they still lost the election. The major political parties, the Democrats, and the Republicans, often work through a very traditional process to endorse candidates. Often a slew of endorsements follows without any real competitive process. The major press outlets often follow a stale and tired campaign evaluation process using campaign financial statements and quick and easy sound bites to sway public opinion. I went on interviews that consisted primarily of questions about my fundraising totals and political connections and little else. I expected journalists to come prepared with hard-hitting interview questions about my personal history, professional accomplishments, educational background, and difficult questions about my political platform. Maybe it was because I was considered a small fry, but this fear never materialized. Half the time, the journalists barely knew my name and that was all. Even in the age of Google, journalists were simply not doing their homework.

BEING AN ALSO-RAN IS BETTER THAN A NEVER-WAS

At the onset of this race, I knew I faced a tremendous uphill battle. I was a poor, single, Latina mother on welfare, out of work, about to be evicted from my apartment running for a race that in years past broke records for the most expense race in the nation's history. Facing a real possibility of homelessness, I was determined to get my name on the ballot come hell or high water. I ran for this position because people like me rarely have our name on the ballot. Representation matters. I did not want the race to be an easy win for anyone. I did not want only the "monied" candidates with the "proper" background and "proper" campaign financing to waltz in and win the office without a fight. I had four goals in my political run. My first mission was to force a run-off and that is exactly what happened. My second goal was to not come in last. I did not come in last. I came in third. Another goal was to surpass 399K votes. The last time a female candidate ran, she received 399K votes. I surpassed that total with a total number of over 980K votes. I was the top vote-getter in one county, Imperial County with 34% of the vote! My final goal was to get a double-digit percentage of votes. Miracle of all miracles, I achieved 16% of the vote. I even received over 20% of the vote in 10 counties across the state of California. So, in the end, I completed all four of my campaign goals. Plus, now I can proudly check off another goal off my bucket list! I got my name on the ballot and ran for political office for reals!

I encourage everyone, to run for office. You are the perfect candidate right now! Politics is about representation, so, go represent! Be a new voice! We need new blood!

Chapter 52

When all is said and done, I cannot express the exhilaration of running as a first-time candidate. The thrill of election night when your name is on the ballot is something unlike anything you can imagine. Even though I came in third in the primary, I know that this is not the last time my name will be on the ballot. This is only the beginning!

Even more importantly, with the general election coming up in November, I cannot emphasize how critical it is for everyone to get out and vote. 2018 is a year where it really does matter! Every vote matters! We cannot make change happen unless we are all represented and all part of the political process.

My final words of advice, I encourage everyone to please get to know the candidates and give a financial contribution. Learn about who is out there. Find out about a candidate or two and help them out! You can volunteer to spread the news about their story and why they are running. Even if you are in another date, go donate to the deserving candidates. I received support from all over the USA! Support the good people who are trying hard to make a difference.

If you are interested in making a positive difference in the world, then register to vote and get out there this November. Every vote is a game changer! Your vote can be the one that wins the game! And this game needs a-changing!

53

We are in a Time of Metamorphosis

Cocooning is staying inside one's home, insulated from perceived danger, instead of going out. The term was coined in 1981 by Faith Popcorn, a trend forecaster and marketing consultant.

Here we go.

No more can we go off naked without a care into the wild blue yonder. With the Covid-19 pandemic, we all are going into the unknown for an unknown amount of time.

Into the cocoon we huddle, as we shelter in place.

How do we cope while we cocoon?

Some people are cocooning and working from home. Many others have lost their jobs and cocooning for survival.

Still, we are all cocooning.

Over the last years from 2020 to 2022, 22 million people were unemployed since the first COVID-19 death in the US. In comparison, during the Great Depression, there were 15 million unemployed after three years. We are truly living in dark, and uncertain times. Experts warn, the worst may be still to come if vaccinations are not mandated.

What then to make of this new cocoon lifestyle?

Being housebound leaves much time to contemplate dreams and goals.

It also produces anxiety and stress over the next phase of life yet to be experienced in the new world once we emerge.

What can we do to prepare for the unimaginable? What to do with all this time?

Health Matters

It goes without saying that we all must make our personal hygiene a top priority now and forever into the future. It means every day we must take extra care with health as it relates to our mental health, nutrition, hygiene, sleep, and exercise. Look for ways to develop your sense and knowledge of what works best for you and your family. Now is the time to learn, grow, and try out new ways of being healthy.

Goal Setting

Now that you are not commuting to work, hassling with dueling personal and professional schedules, and life's comfortable daily routine is only a faint memory, you need new goals and new aspirations. Perhaps you have always wanted to write a book or maybe learn a musical instrument or learn a foreign language. Before you set goals check in with who you are today in 2022. Check in with the world that is the world of 2022. You are no longer who you were before the pandemic. Your goals should not be from a world that has completely and totally changed. Set goals based on heading into a very different post-Covid world. Create 2 or 3 short- and long-term goals for 2 weeks out, 2 months out, 6 months out, and one year out. Our new self and the world of work will be operating from the cocoon for a while.

Take Inventory

A cocoon is self-sufficient. The caterpillar does not peep its head out for even one second. The cocoon cannot work if it is interrupted because you run out of toilet paper, medicine, or supplies. Do you need to set up your home office? Do you need a new router? Do you need a clean wall behind your desk for online conference calls/interviews? Do you need a new can opener? Do you need to learn to cook? It is time to settle into your cocoon and become self-sufficient. We will be home for quite a while. Be prepared to settle into the process.

Self-compassion

Self-care is tossed around a lot these days. It can be understood as the protection of one's well-being and happiness. Often it is believed that self-care is the most important part of healthy living, but self-compassion is equally important in times of crises. Kristin Neff has defined self-compassion as being composed of three main components – self-kindness, common humanity, and mindfulness. Giving self-compassion to yourself will help you to develop compassion for others, especially if you are responsible for providing care for those dealing with sickness. Build relationships with yourself and others to help you through these dark times.

Cocooning does not mean life comes to a standstill. On the contrary. We, all of us, are in the process of a complete metamorphosis. Self, society, and the world.

Our lives are changing and will continue to change as we work our way out of the pandemic.

But we can choose to prepare and participate in the transformation process from inside our own cocoon.

One day it will be time to leave the cocoon.

We will stretch out our wings.

And off we will soar into the wild blue yonder.

References

American College Health Association. (2012). ACHA guidelines: Standards of practice for health promotion in higher education. https://www.naspa.org/images/uploads/kcs/WHPL_Canon_HP_Standards_of_Practice_for_Health_Promotion_in_Higher_Education_May2012.pdf

Ames, E. (2014). Concept of High-Level Wellness. http://www.wwu.edu/wwura/pdf/0911.pdf

Ansell-Pearson, K., & Schrift, A. D. (2014). Henri Bergson. In *The New Century* (pp. 37-64). Routledge.

Antonovsky, A. (1987). *Unraveling the mystery of health: How people manage stress and stay well*. Jossey-bass.

Blum, R. W. (2005). A case for school connectedness. *Educational Leadership, 62*(7), 16-20.

Bowlby, J. (2008). *Attachment*. Basic books.

Bronfenbrenner, U. (1979). *The ecology of human development*. Harvard University Press.

Brown, A. (2019). From Cultural Competency to Liberation: Incorporating healing-centered pedagogy to foster sense of belonging. Georgia State University.

Caldwell, R. and Wilt, K. (2019). Holistic Nutrition for Student Health and Sustainable Food Policy. University of South Carolina.

Carney, C. E., Edinger, J. D., Meyer, B., Lindman, L., & Istre, T. (2006). Daily activities and sleep quality in college students. *Chronobiology international, 23*(3), 623-637.

Changing Minds (2018). Type A and Type B. http://changingminds.org/explanations/preferences/typea_typeb.htm.

Charter, O. (2013). An international charter for health promoting universities and colleges. (2015). In *An outcome of the 2015 International Conference on Health Promoting Universities and Colleges/VII International Congress* (pp. 1-12). https://www.naspa.org/images/uploads/kcs/WHPL_Ca non_HP_Okanagan_Charter_12.pdf

Christens, B. D., & Inzeo, P. T. (2015). Widening the view: situating collective impact among frameworks for community-led change. *Community Development*, 46(4), 420-435. https://www.naspa.org/images/uploads/kcs/Widening_the_view_situating_collective_impact_among_frameworks_for_community_led_change_-_2015.pdf

Council for the Advancement of Standards (2019). Retrieved on March 16, 2019. https://www.cas.edu/

Dooris, M. (2010). Healthy Universities: Introduction and Model. Royal Society of Public Health.\

Csikszentmihalyi, M., Abuhamdeh, S., & Nakamura, J. (2014). Flow. In *Flow and the foundations of positive psychology* (pp. 227-238). Springer, Dordrecht.

Deci, E. L., & Ryan, R. M. (Eds.). (2004). *Handbook of self-determination research*. University Rochester Press.

Diener, E. (1984). Subjective well-being. *Psychological bulletin*, 95(3), 542.

Edinger, J. D., Wohlgemuth, W. K., Radtke, R. A., Marsh, G. R., & Quillian, R. E. (2001). Does cognitive-behavioral insomnia therapy alter dysfunctional beliefs about sleep?. *Sleep*, 24(5), 591-599.

Eisenberg, N., & Strayer, J. (Eds.). (1990). *Empathy and its development*. CUP Archive.

Emmons, R. A., & McCullough, M. E. (Eds.). (2004). *The psychology of gratitude*. Oxford University Press.

Engelhard Pingree, S. and Harward, D. W. (2013). The Well-being and Flourishing of Students. https://www.naspa.org/images/uploads/kcs/WHPL_Canon_WB_BTtoPWell-beingInitiative.pdf

Eriksson, M., & Lindström, B. (2007). Antonovsky's sense of coherence scale and its relation with quality of life: a systematic review. *Journal of Epidemiology & Community Health*, 61(11), 938-944.

Freire, P., & Freire, A. M. A. (2004). *EPZ pedagogy of hope: Reliving pedagogy of the oppressed*. A&C Black.

Goleman, D. (2006). *Emotional intelligence*. Bantam.

Goodwin, J. L., Kaemingk, K. L., Fregosi, R. F., Rosen, G. M., Morgan, W. J., Smith, T., & Quan, S. F. (2004). Parasomnias and sleep disordered breathing in Caucasian and Hispanic children–the Tucson children's assessment of sleep apnea study. *BMC medicine*, 2(1), 14.

Harmat, L., Takács, J., & Bodizs, R. (2008). Music improves sleep quality in students. *Journal of advanced nursing*, 62(3), 327-335.

https://www.naspa.org/images/uploads/kcs/WHPL_Canon_HP_Dooris_2010_HU-Intro_Model.pdf

https://www.naspa.org/images/uploads/kcs/WHPL_Canon_Le_Leadership_for_a_Healthy_Campus-36.pdf

https://www.naspa.org/images/uploads/kcs/WHPL_Canon_We_Wellness_Its_orgins_Theories_and_applications.pdf

Irwin, M. R., Olmstead, R., & Motivala, S. J. (2008). Improving sleep quality in older adults with moderate sleep complaints: a randomized controlled trial of Tai Chi Chih. *Sleep, 31*(7), 1001-1008.

Jarrin, D. C., McGrath, J. J., Silverstein, J. E., & Drake, C. (2013). Objective and subjective socioeconomic gradients exist for sleep quality, sleep latency, sleep duration, weekend oversleep, and daytime sleepiness in adults. *Behavioral sleep medicine, 11*(2), 144-158.

Jensen, B. B., & Schnack, K. (1994). Action competence as an educational challenge. In *Action and action competence as key concepts in critical pedagogy* (pp. 5-18). Danmarks Lærerhøjskole.

Kegan, R. (1994). In over our heads: The mental complexity of modern life.

Lewin, K. (1936). *Principles of Topological Psychology*. New York: McGraw-Hill.

Lichstein, K. L., Riedel, B. W., Wilson, N. M., Lester, K. W., & Aguillard, R. N. (2001). Relaxation and sleep compression for late-life insomnia: a placebo-controlled trial. *Journal of consulting and clinical psychology, 69*(2), 227.

Love, A. G. (2013). Wagner College: Establishing Positive Links between Civic Engagement and Student Well-being.

Lozano, J. (2019). Tools for FYE Students to Deal with Emotional Problems. Monterrey Technical Institute.

Manjunath, N. K., & Telles, S. (2005). Influence of Yoga & Ayurveda on self-rated sleep in a geriatric population. *Indian Journal of Medical Research, 121*(5), 683.

Michigan State University (2019) Retrieved on March 16, 2019. https://olin.msu.edu/aboutus/history.htm

National Association of Student Personnel Administrators' Health Education and Leadership Program. (2005). Leadership for a Healthy Campus, An Ecological Approach for Student Success.

Obear, K. (2019). Self-Care and Healing as Campus Change Agents: Renew, rejuvenate, and recommit. Social Justice Training Institute.

Pallesen, S., Saxvig, I. W., Molde, H., Sørensen, E., Wilhelmsen-Langeland, A., & Bjorvatn, B. (2011). Brief report: behaviorally induced insufficient sleep syndrome in older adolescents: prevalence and correlates. *Journal of adolescence, 34*(2), 391-395.

Pascarella, E., & Terenzini, P. (1997). Pattern of Student–Faculty Interaction Beyond the Classroom and Voluntary Freshman Attrition. *Journal of College Student Development, 32*, 123-130.

Porter, V. (2019) A Mind-body Prescription for Restful Sleep. Retrieved on March 19, 2019. https://chopra.com/articles/mind-body-perscription-restful-sleep

Raymond, J. (2018). http://www.drjeanetteraymond.com retrieved on March 1, 2018.

Schroeder, C. C. (1999). Partnerships: An imperative for enhancing student learning and institutional effectiveness. *New Directions for Student Services, 1999*(87), 5-18.

Schuder, K. (2018). Understanding the Type A Personality.

Scott, E. (2018). Type A Stress relief tips. https://www.verywellmind.com/type-a-stress-relief-3145058 Wolf, D.A. (2014). How to relax (When you're a type A Personality)

Seligman, M. E. (2006). *Learned optimism: How to change your mind and your life*. Vintage.

Soeffing, J. P., Lichstein, K. L., Nau, S. D., McCrae, C. S., Wilson, N. M., Aguillard, R. N., & Bush, A. J. (2008). Psychological treatment of insomnia in hypnotic-dependent older adults. *Sleep Medicine, 9*(2), 165-171.

Springer, F., & Phillips, J. L. (2006). The IOM model: A tool for prevention planning and implementation. *Prevention Tactics, 8*(13), 1-8. https://www.naspa.org/images/uploads/kcs/WHPL_Canon_Pr_Prevention_Tactics_Springer_8.pdf

Stará, J., & Charvát, M. (2015). Wellness: Its Origins, Theories and Current Applications in the United States. *Acta Salus Vitae, 1*(2).

Strange & Banning. (2015). Designing for Learning: Creating Campus Environments for Student Success. Jossey-Bass. San Francisco, CA 94104-1342.

Thelin, J. R. (2011). *A history of American higher education*. JHU Press.

Vincent, D., & Lewycky, S. E. (2009). Research Forum. *Behavior Therapist, 32*(6).

Waters, F., & Bucks, R. S. (2011). Neuropsychological effects of sleep loss: implication for neuropsychologists. *Journal of the International Neuropsychological Society, 17*(4), 571-586.

Waters, F., & Bucks, R. S. (2011). Neuropsychological effects of sleep loss: implication for neuropsychologists. *Journal of the International Neuropsychological Society, 17*(4), 571-586.

Wellman, D. (2019) Strategies for Building Intention and Coherence in Peer Leadership. University of South Carolina.

World Health Organization. (1986). Ottawa Charter for Health Promotion. https://www.who.int/healthpromotion/conferences/previous/ottawa/en/

Zimmerman, M. A. (1990). Toward a theory of learned hopefulness: A structural model analysis of participation and empowerment. *Journal of research in personality, 24*(1), 71-86.

Online Resources

8 Dimensions of Wellness, https://rm.edu/blog/the-8-dimensions-of-wellness/

Being Human in STEM, http://www.beinghumaninstem.com/

Beyond Consent, https://www.hopkinsmedicine.org/news/publications/hopkins_medicine_magazine/hopkins_reader/fall-2018/beyond-consent-seeking-justice-in-research

Bystander Intervention, https://www.ihollaback.org/bystander-resources/

Environmental Sustainability, Earlham College, https://earlham.edu/academics/majors-minors-programs/environmental-sustainability/

First-Year Experience, University of South Carolina, https://sc.edu/about/offices_and_divisions/national_resource_center/events/conferences/first-year_experience/

Friend 2 Friend Suicide Prevention, https://www.sprc.org/resources-programs/friend2friend

Habitudes, https://growingleaders.com/habitudes/

Health Education Awareness Resource Team (HEART) Peer Educator, https://wellness.temple.edu/peer-education

Healthy Minds Network, https://healthymindsnetwork.org/research/data-for-researchers/

MyPlate, USDA, https://www.myplate.gov/

PAC 201 Relaxation, Oregon State University, https://health.oregonstate.edu/pac/class/pac-201-relaxation

PSYC E-1019 Stress, Coping, and Resilience, Harvard University, https://courses.dce.harvard.edu/?keyword=25196&srcdb=202202?utm_source=olp&utm_medium=referral&utm_campaign=spr22

Puente Project, https://www.thepuenteproject.org/

Restorative Justice,

http://restorativejustice.org/#sthash.jNH81Gxk.JAnuQQTl.dpbs

UC Healthy Campus Initiative, https://globalfood.ucr.edu/gfi-projects/healthy-campus-initiative

Umoja Community Program, https://umojacommunity.org/our-story

University of Pennsylvania, Master of Applied Positive Psychology, https://www.lps.upenn.edu/degree-programs/mapp

About the Author

Lily E. Espinoza (Ploski), the author of *Not Getting Stuck: Success stories of Being Latina and Transferring from a California community college,* is the host of the YouTube series Lily College Mythbusters, is a nationally recognized speaker on college choice and is a volunteer for community organizations and boards including the Solano Food Bank, Benicia PTA, Solano County Women and Girls Commission and served as past vice-chair on the City of Benicia Arts and Culture Commission and past vice-chair with the non-profit My New Red Shoes. Lily, is a 2nd generation immigrant Latina with family from Culiacán, Sinaloa, Mexico with Mayo indigenous roots, and her Polish family is by way of Waterbury, Connecticut. Dr. Espinoza has been featured on public radio KPFA *La Raza* Chronicles. Lily hikes, rollerskates, hot tubs, and nurtures herself in the San Francisco Bay Area, native lands of the Patwin people, and is a single mother to her son, Justice, and his black cat named Bili.

ABOOKS

ALIVE Book Publishing and ALIVE Publishing Group
are imprints of Advanced Publishing LLC,
3200 A Danville Blvd., Suite 204, Alamo, California 94507

925.837.7303
alivebookpublishing.com

www.ingramcontent.com/pod-product-compliance
Lightning Source LLC
Chambersburg PA
CBHW020352170426
43200CB00005B/144